THE ASKING

BOOKS BY JANE HIRSHfiELD

JANE HIRSHFIELD

The Asking

NEW & SELECTED POEMS

BLOODAXE BOOKS

Copyright © Jane Hirshfield 2023, 2024

ISBN: 978 1 78037 679 0

First published in the UK in 2024 by
Bloodaxe Books Ltd,
Eastburn,
South Park,
Hexham,
Northumberland NE46 1BS.

First published in the USA in 2023 by Alfred A. Knopf, Inc.

www.bloodaxebooks.com
For further information about Bloodaxe titles
please visit our website and join our mailing list
or write to the above address for a catalogue.

Supported using public funding by
ARTS COUNCIL
ENGLAND

LEGAL NOTICE
All rights reserved. No part of this book may be
reproduced, stored in a retrieval system, or
transmitted in any form, or by any means, electronic,
mechanical, photocopying, recording or otherwise,
without prior written permission from Bloodaxe Books Ltd.

Requests to publish work from this book
must be sent to Bloodaxe Books Ltd.

Jane Hirshfield has asserted her right under
Section 77 of the Copyright, Designs and Patents Act 1988
to be identified as the author of this work.

Poems from previously published books used by permission of Jane Hirshfield and with thanks
to Quarterly Review of Literature Poetry Series for *Alaya* (1982), to Wesleyan University Press
for *Of Gravity & Angels* (1988), and to HarperCollins Publishers for *The October Palace*
(1994), *The Lives of the Heart* (1997) and *Given Sugar, Given Salt* (2001); and by permission
of Jane Hirshfield and Bloodaxe Books Ltd for poems from *Each Happiness Ringed by Lions*
(2005), *After* (2006), *Come, Thief* (2012), *The Beauty* (2015) and *Ledger* (2020). The epigraph
from Yehuda Amichai (p.105) was translated by Yehuda Amichai and Ted Hughes. The
epigraphs from Dante (p.99) and Praxilla (p.87) are in English versions by Jane Hirshfield.

Cover design: Neil Astley & Pamela Robertson-Pearce.

Printed in Great Britain by Bell & Bain Limited, Glasgow, Scotland, on
acid-free paper sourced from mills with FSC chain of custody certification.

CONTENTS

FROM *The October Palace* (1994)

FROM *The Lives of the Heart* (1988)

FROM *Given Sugar, Given Salt* (2001)

FROM *After* (2006)

❧

FROM *Come, Thief* (2011)

FROM *The Beauty* (2015)

New Poems

(2023)

DOOR AND SENTENCE

My life,
you were a door I was given
to walk through.

Dawdling
in lintel and loosestrife as much as permitted.

Your own glass knob,
I spoke you:

A sentence, however often rewritten,
ending always with the same slightly rusty-hinged preposition,
sometimes, for mercy, hidden.

COUNTING, NEW YEAR'S MORNING,
WHAT POWERS YET REMAIN TO ME

The world asks, as it asks daily:
And what can you make, can you do, to change my deep-broken, fractured?

I count, this first day of another year, what remains.
I have a mountain, a kitchen, two hands.

Can admire with two eyes the mountain,
actual, recalcitrant, shuffling its pebbles, sheltering foxes and beetles.

Can make black-eyed peas and collards.
Can make, from last year's late-ripening persimmons, a pudding.
Can climb a stepladder, change the bulb in a track light.

For years, I woke each day first to the mountain,
then to the question.

The feet of the new sufferings followed the feet of the old,
and still they surprised.

I brought salt, brought oil, to the question. Brought sweet tea,
brought postcards and stamps. For years, each day, something.

Stone did not become apple. War did not become peace.
Yet joy still stays joy. Sequins stay sequins. Words still bespangle, bewilder.

Today, I woke without answer.

The day answers, unpockets a thought as though from a friend—

don't despair of this falling world, not yet   didn't it give you the asking

TIN

I studied much and remembered little.
But the world is generous, it kept offering figs and cheeses.
Never mind that soon I'll have to give it all back,
the world, the figs.
To be a train station of existence is no small matter.
It doesn't need to be Grand Central or Haydarpaşa Station.
The engine shed could be low, windowed with coal dust
under a slat-shingled roof. It could be tin.
Another mystery bandaged with rivets and rubies.
Leaking cold and heat in both directions, as the earth does.

MANIFEST

Hawks, rivers, cities, ochre, us.

A species whose right hand sketches its left hand
but can't draw itself.

Whales.
Geosynchronous satellites.
A truck hauling folded tarps under a tarp.

Wars, hunger, jail cells, praises, pratfalls, puns,
gold circuits on phone-card connectors—
all cargo, manifest,
            circling the sun together
each three hundred and sixty-five days
plus a few remnant hours.

A story here ribboned with lightning,
there dimmed by clouds,
on a nitrogen-, oxygen-,
carbon-dioxide-, and dust-cushioned bundle,
whose glaciers depart, insects quiet, seas rise.

To that which is coming, I say,
Here, take what is yours.

But forget, if you can, what-is-coming,
find not worth pocketing,
let fall unnoticed as weed seed,
one small handful of moments and gestures.

Moments mouse-colored, minor.
Gestures disturbing no one,
slipped between the ones that were counted,
the ones in which everything happened.

A petroglyph's single fingerprint.

A spider awake in an undusted corner.

Let stay, if you can, what-is-coming,
one or two musical notes,
hummed in a half hour that couldn't be herded
or mined,
made to save daylight or spend it.

Leave one unfraudulent hope,
one affection like curtains blown open in wind,
whose minutes, seconds, fragrance,
choices,
won't sadden the heart to recall.

SOLSTICE

The Earth today tilts one way, then another.

And yes, though all things change,
this night again will watch its fireflies,
then go in to a bed with sheets,
to lights, a beloved.

To running water cold and hot.

Take nothing for granted,
you who were also opulent, a stung cosmos.

Birds sing, frogs sing, their *sufficient unto*.
The late-night rain-bringing thunder.

And if days grow ordinarily shorter,
the dark's mirror lengthens,

and one's gain is not the other lessened.

TWO VERSIONS

In the first version I slept by a stream.

All night awake things traveled near.

One jumped—large-of-belly & startled—straight over.
One walked, small-clawed, across my open palm.

What was my palm doing, I now wonder,
outside the sleeping bag, facing the fathoms of air,
by a common watering hole in a creature-summoning night?

Was it curious? lonely?

And why, when I conjure a lifetime of ignorance,
miscalculation, misjudgments,
do I think, of all possible choices, of this?

In the second version, there is only their thirst,
of which I knew nothing.

Except to have been in the way of.

All night, so many thirsty. In strong darkness.
Forty years, and I am still begging pardon.

TODAY, WHEN I COULD DO NOTHING

Today, when I could do nothing,
I saved an ant.

It must have come in with the morning paper,
still being delivered
to those who shelter in place.

A morning paper is still an essential service.

I am not an essential service.

I have coffee and books,
time,
a garden,
silence enough to fill cisterns.

It must have first walked
the morning paper, as if loosened ink
taking the shape of an ant.

Then across the laptop computer—warm—
then onto the back of a cushion.

Small black ant, alone,
crossing a navy cushion,
moving steadily because that is what it could do.

Set outside in the sun,
it could not have found again its nest.
What then did I save?

It did not look as if it was frightened,
even while walking my hand,
which moved it through swiftness and air.

Ant, alone, without companions,
whose ant-heart I could not fathom—
how is your life, I wanted to ask.

I lifted it, took it outside.

This first day when I could do nothing,
contribute nothing
beyond staying distant from my own kind,
I did this.

March 17, 2020

POEM HOLDING A WRISTWATCH BELONGING
TO THE BRAZILIAN POET FERREIRA GULLAR

I've been waiting to find again my own right proportion.
So often, a person's size is too big.
Less often, too small.
Either you block the view completely
or you stand peering, squinting, one small hand
shielding your face from the sun.
Sometimes I stand next to trees
hoping to earn my arms' reach around them. Sometimes,
a horse. You can't find your right size at all next to other people,
and never next to an ant,
to whom you can only apologize for being clumsy and cumbersome.
Also, loud. I've never heard an ant shouting, yet everything
an ant wants to do seems to get done.
The moment I do feel myself holding a spoon even-handedly,
balanced by fingers and thumb,
while sitting precisely upright in a human-sized chair,
size escapes me entirely. Also, time does.
I'm inside a day measured by wrist and not wristwatch.
The words *size* and *time* keep turning themselves into laughter,
something you do with *self* and *air*, which turn into laughter also.
Like cutting the dough of this world to bake into birds that are already
    flying.

EACH MORNING CALLS US TO PRAISE
THIS WORLD THAT IS FLEETING

Each morning
waking
amidst the not-ever-before,
dressing inside the not-ever-again.

Under sunlight or cloud,
brushing the hair.

Not yet arrived
at the end-crimped finish,
drinking coffee
and buttering toast.

Permitted to slip into coat, into shoes,
I go out,
I count myself part,

carrying only
a weightless shadow,
whose each corner joins and departs
from the shadows of others.

Mortal, alive among others
equally fragile.

And with luck—
for days even, sometimes—
this luxury, this extra gift:

able to even forget it.

TWO KEROSENE LANTERNS

The cat walks the narrow shelf beneath the window
where many delicate things are arranged—polished ammonites,
a dried starfish, three turtle netsuke,
a few curls of birch bark, two long-unused kerosene lanterns.

As if on their own, two hands fly up to cover the person's face,
to cover the eyes already closed.

The crash, as it must, arrives.

The hands lower slowly.
The cat sits on the floor in the room's middle, calmly licking one paw.

The law of cats is simple: one arrangement becomes another.

People are strange.

TO BE A PERSON

To be a person is an untenable proposition.

Odd of proportion,
upright,
unbalanced of body, feeling, and mind.

Two predators' eyes
face forward,
yet seem always to be trying to look back.

Unhooved, untaloned fingers
seem to grasp mostly grief and pain.
To create, too often, mostly grief and pain.

Some take,
in witnessed suffering, pleasure.
Some make, of witnessed suffering, beauty.

On the other side—
a creature capable of blushing,
who chooses to spin until dizzy,
likes what is shiny,
demands to stay awake even when sleepy.

Learns what is basic, what acid,
what are stomata, nuclei, jokes,
which birds are flightless.
Learns to play four-handed piano.
To play, when it is needed, one-handed piano.

Hums. Feeds strays.
Says, "All together now, on three."

To be a person may be possible then, after all.

Or the question may be considered still at least open—
an unused drawer, a pair of waiting workboots.

O, RESPONSIBILITY

On one side,
irretrievable spires and cobbles,
ladders, arpeggios,
boletes, apples, oysters,
lists and languages lost under sand.

On the other,
what can be wrestled with still,
reconnoitered,
returned to, repaired.

O, responsibility!
Tied to the feast of your stanchion
like a tired donkey.

With commensurate ears
one could hear the old music in you—

some June-singing thrush

or distant,
one-stringed instrument,
made of maple wood, rabbit skin, horse hair—

neither separate from nor completing the cries of the famished.

Here & Now

try to describe it

even one quick line
drawn with unlifted pencil

already wrong

Words Stop

Words stop.
A great tenderness rises.

Why do I set this down now in words?

My Failure

I said of the view: "Just some trees."

Chrysanthemum

it doesn't need to know   its own fragrance

Vestment

for the pear, for the fig,
no difference

they ripen

even in ashfall

A DAY JUST ENDS

for H.H. (1922–2020)

A day just ends.

Its dusk comes simply,
without opinion or hesitation.

A fork still fits hand,
shoes fit feet,
on this day, like any other.

She closed her eyes,
opened her mouth
to receive the end of her life.

Its last tasting.

I ASKED TO BE LUSH, TO BE GREEN.

I pressed myself to the clear glass
between wanting and world.

I wanted to be lush, tropical,
excessive. To be green.

On the glass that does not exist,
small breath-clouds rose, dissolved.

A creature of water, I found myself.

Tender, still also of air.

The dry bark of trees
sequestered the hidden rising.

I told my grief: patience.
I offered my want the old promise—

a tree not wet to the touch is wet to the living.

"A MAP GROWS NO TREES."

—Alberto Blanco

Yet a thought is a forest.
Birds knock their heads against living tree trunks,
looking for living beetles.

This continual concussion
must be why sureties so often confuse.

Moss on the north side, leaves going up,
roots going down,
and still for a lifetime I've kept getting lost.

THERMOPOLIUM

Found in an earthenware vessel,
remnants of a Pompeiian street stand's last-day stew:
fish, sheep meat, snails.

Perhaps a meal delicious, tender.
The archaeologist doesn't say.

A person eats first for the joy of tasting,
then for the joy
of living to be once again hungry.

A person tilts the head
when they hear or see something new,
as if change of angle could lead
to a change of seeing.

But eats with the head
held upright, untilted,
directly above the reliable throat, stomach,
intestines, legs, feet.

Eats with the life that expects to go on.

Then something surprises—
a recipe, or the end of the world as you've known it—
and you pause, mouth filled with fish, snails, and sheep meat,
tilt your head to listen one moment longer.

THE DIFFICULT DAY

Looking through the difficult day to see the mountain,
I heard:

"Through"? No. You are making an error.

Whose voice this ontological protest—
the day's? the mountain's? some distant piano or hawk?—
I couldn't tell.

Only that it stepped between suffering and suffering,
like a rock
going through a window before it has broken.

POEM TO BE WRITTEN BY MAGNET
IN OIL FOR AN EXHIBIT AT THE MUSEUM
OF TOMORROW IN RIO DE JANEIRO

Today, I think I'll join an exiled Italian poet,
perhaps Ovid or Horace,
training a handful of grape vines on a steep-sided farm.

You don't need a not-yet-invented machine to do that.
Words make time's saddle.
The horse's back rises and falls, going away.

Or I'll join the vines. I'll drink the sun straight,
as they do.

Vines, unlike poets, don't talk much,
or struggle with what they're turning a lifetime into.
They turn their big leaves, and grapes just arrive.

A human heart, sent into exile from all its wanting,
might ripen like that,
into some small-clustered kindness or a rescuing joke.

The way a magnet becomes itself wherever there's iron.
Plunged into water, set into oil, it still pulls.

A magnet doesn't have to go into exile to be a magnet.
Put a magnet down anywhere on this earth,
that magnet is home.

BODY, MIND OF THE RANSACKED THRIFT SHOP

Body, mind of the ransacked thrift shop:
I here bequeath you.

Knees: yellowing articles clipped from the news.
Blood: mosquitoes reject it.
Closets: time now to empty. Books: go.

Like an old dog, I'll find my one exactly-dog-sized pond of sun.
I'll sleep, I'll swim.

I'll keep with me
only one habit too hard to lose: I'll still bark at what passes.

SILENCE: AN ASSAY

No one wants to buy you, or gossip about you,
or play your unlabeled, unlined vinyl LP.
How quickly you're consigned to the bin labeled boredom.
How untradeable, how unfollowed down a dark street.
Silence cannot be taught and refuses all invitations.
Cupped in one open hand, it feels weightless.
With time, though, silence starts to grow heavy, to silently weep.
But it's hard to be silent while weeping;
the silence leaves. The empty hand, without it,
trembles a little. Einstein called time what stops everything
from happening at once. Silence stops everything
from shouting at once. At 5:18 here every morning,
one loud bird complains about too much silence.
The day is here, the day is here, it announces.
No other birds join it, so it goes back to being quiet.
Hearing it helps me. Each morning I'm
glad of silence, but also glad of the bird
that woke me so I can be happy a moment
right alongside it, knowing soon I'll again not be awake.
Silence is generous, that way. Also: is poor.
It's worth nothing, until you'd give anything for some.

MY WINDOW

Age also of maples,
still wearing their big-handed leaves.
Of cotoneaster, red again with new-mustered berries.
Of sunlight and shadow, trapeze-artist squirrels.

Once, a one-day blizzard of
birds whose bodies' feathered enamels gleamed.

It isn't hunger, this looking.
It isn't thirst.

The eyes just want to see what they will be leaving,
the way birds flock to eat what will be gone

because they have eaten.

INVITATION

It was not given me to write in the primary colors.
I did not recognize the 350,000 species of beetle.
I loved what was spare but could not draw it.
My luck and errors equally mostly escaped me.
My eyes faltered, but found their way to different windows.
The fate-souk bartered my shapes and sounds between stalls.
When the keyboard offered an incomprehensible symbol,
I reached my hand out, as if to a Ouija board's invitation
or a stair's polished handrail, because it was incomprehensible,
because my hand could add its own oils to that railing.

Again, I enter my life.
Calligraphed each day newly,
in a language
strange to me, awkward,
its letters and etymologies,
even its ink unfamiliar.
Its hours set in a country
where others walk
side by side
sure of direction,
appearing to know
which shop they're considering,
and if it's tomatoes,
shoes, or aspirin
they're wanting to buy.
On the subway maps,
shapes and colors
are clear, but not
the names of the stations.
My ears refuse their conductor,
my feet move toward
each slid-open door.
Each day it grows harder to say
how all this happened
and continues to happen.
Perhaps some changed life
is attempting to enter me,
the way clay and wheel
turn the hands of the potter
into the hands of a potter.
Nor is my life
addressed with a singular pronoun.
Its *I* a fish-school
of mutual, fellow-traveling
incomprehensions,
its *you* demanding always

the plural and formal,
its *he / she / it*
taking an oddly specialized
somehow subjective grammar,
not theirs, not mine.
The verb tense?
Past future imperfect.
The weather?
Though already changing,
still bearably humid,
hospitable, even,
to a multi-cellular flock
that each night forgets entirely
how it should waken—
into a story, into a self,
or a murmuration.

MOSSES

In the Mojave Desert, a translucent crystal offers bryophytes much-needed respite from the heat of the sun.

—*The New York Times*, July 29, 2020

For hypolithic mosses,
it seems,
four percent of daylight is right.
They live, the headline says,
by sheltering
under a parasol of translucent quartz.

The crystal scatters
the light's ultraviolet,
dilutes its heat,
traps the night's condensed moisture
to moss-sized rain.

I think of these mosses
and consider.
Perhaps we, too, are mosses,
evolving to the parch
of our self-made Mojaves.

Unable to bear the full brightness,
the full seeing.

To recognize fully the Amazon burning,
the Arctic burning,
the monarchs' smoke-colored missing migration.

An experiment not meant to last.

And yet we found shelter within it,
we pondered our lives and the lives of others,
thirsted, slept.

To the implausible green of existence,
for-better, for-worse,
we offered our four-percent portion of praises,

for-better, for-worse,
our four-percent portion of comprehension.

LETTER TO ADAM ZAGAJEWSKI

(1945–2021)

As if walking the Old Town of Kraków
in one quick half-hour
in the midst of a lengthening conversation—
in one afternoon and an evening, a life's work can be read.

Of all you had hoped for, much did arrive.

A new saeculum opened—however briefly—its windows.
You loved and were loved.
Your poems became themselves fully.
Also, more sad.

The yearning for birds, animals, insects, cities, mystics,
stayed for a lifetime.

To them, you compared many things—

The wind yawned for you once like a foxhound.
Dusk spoke in Sanskrit.

You noted, calmly, the earth's indifference,
then noted its chestnut trees' openings, summonings, calls.

You lived in three countries, carried three countries' passports.
Time stamped onto each of their pages
its visas' ornate, colored inks:
griefs, loves, meals, musics, haircuts.

Is it now—already so quickly?—for you
as you once imagined for poets then already dead?

"Their doubts vanished with them," you wrote.
"Their rapture lives."

AUBADE NOW OF EARTH

Sun on it again, at first tender.
The color of apricots ripening into.

At first there was more to eat, then suddenly less.

For one night only, naked in my arms,
wrote Beatriz of Dia, in twelfth-century Occitan,
to her longed-for lover.

Aubade now of earth. Of water. Of herons and fishes.

Dawn after dawn one night only, we woke in your arms.

I WOULD LIKE

I would like
my living to inhabit me
the way
rain, sun, and their wanting
inhabit a fig or an apple.

I would like to meet my life
also in pieces,
scattered:
a conversation set down
on a long hallway table;

a disappointment
pocketed inside a jacket;
some long-ago longing glimpsed,
half-recognized,
in the corner of a thrift store painting.

To discover my happiness,
walking first
toward
then away from me
down a stairwell,
on two strong legs all its own.

Also,
the uncountable
wheat stalks,
how many times broken,
beaten, sent
between grindstones,
before entering
the marriage
of oven and bread—

Let me find my life in that, too.

In my moments
of clumsiness, solitude;
in days of vertigo and hesitation;
in the many year-ends
that found me
standing on top of a stovetop
to take down a track light.

In my nights' asked,
sometimes answered, questions.

I would like
to add to my life,
while we are still living,
a little salt and butter,
one more slice of the edible apple,
a teaspoon of jam
from the long-simmered fig.

To taste
as if something tasted for the first time
what we will have become then.

I OPEN THE WINDOW.

What I wanted
wasn't to let in the wetness.
That can be mopped.

Nor the cold.
There are blankets.

What I wanted was
the siren, the thunder, the neighbor,
the fireworks, the dog's bark.

Which of them didn't matter?

Yes, this world is perfect,
all things as they are.

But I wanted
not to be
the one sleeping soundly, on a soft pillow,
clean sheets untroubled,
dreaming there still might be time,

while this everywhere crying

Alaya

(1971–1982)

AND / YES IN THE FIELDS YOU

And
yes in the fields you
must wind for me
ropes of wheatstalk
weave me walls
out of husked corn ears
and the shed skins
of a reptile's turnings
in the soil   yes & I
will lend you years
of water
fins to bend them
to a circle and to mirrors
of my eyes the sun white
blinding hard behind the shutters
and oh
yes this clapboard house
these rooms cool leaning
each against the other
like a picket fence in spring

(1971)

DECEMBER SOLSTICE, '73

The days will be getting longer now.
Outside it is raining and raining.

We spoke so much with the same voice,
how will they tell us apart?
One voice, many mouths,
we are many even alone.

But when the time came,
it darkened & rained through my tongue.

My sleep has the texture of canvas, waiting.
You go out to the streets,
and try to bargain,
driving your life like a nail, deep into time.

I was wrong:
we were foreigners in the same country,
trying to weep.

And learning ourselves
like a hard to decipher book,
we will each come away with separate meanings,
friend.

EVERYTHING THAT IS NOT YOU

One gain, one loss,
whatever is said.
And the light streaming in
through Venetian blinds.

As this room could be any room,
these words any words.

The impossible closes around
like a smooth lake
on an early morning swim:
everything that is not you.

FROM

Of Gravity & Angels

(1988)

AFTER WORK

I stop the car along the pasture edge,
gather up bags of corncobs from the back,
and get out.
Two whistles, one for each,
and familiar sounds draw close in darkness—
cadence of hoof on hardened bottomland,
twinned blowing of air through nostrils curious, flared.
They come, deepened and muscular movements
conjured out of sleep: each small noise and scent
heavy with earth, simple beyond communion,
beyond the stretched out hand from which they calmly
take corncobs, pulling away as I hold
until the mid-points snap.
They are careful of my fingers,
offering that animal-knowledge,
the respect which is due to strangers;
and in the night, their mares' eyes shine, reflecting stars,
the entire, outer light of the world here.

IN A NET OF BLUE AND GOLD

When the moored boat lifts, for its moment,
out of the water like a small cloud—
this is when I understand.
It floats there, defying the stillness to break,
its white hull doubled on the surface smooth as glass.
A minor miracle, utterly purposeless.
Even the bird on the bow-line takes it in stride,
barely shifting his weight before resuming
whatever musing it is birds do;
and the fish continue their placid, mid-day
truce with the world, suspended a few feet below.
I catch their gleam, the jeweled, reflecting scales,
small dragons guarding common enough treasure.
And wonder how, bound to each other as we are
in a net of blue and gold,
we fail so often, in such ordinary ways.

INVOCATION

This August night, raccoons,
come to the back door
burnished all summer by salty,
human touch: enter secretly & eat.

Listen, little mask-faced ones,
unstealthy bandits whose tails
are barred with dusk:
listen, gliding green-eyed ones:
I concede you gladly
all this much-handled stuff,
garbage, grain,
the cropped food and cropped heart—
may you gnaw in contentment
through the sleep-hours
on everything left out.

May you find the house
hospitable,
well-used,
stocked with sufficient goods.
I'll settle with your leavings,

as you have settled for mine,
before startling back into darkness
that marks each of us so differently.

Only if I move my arm a certain way,
it comes back.
Or the way the light bends in the trees
this time of year,
so a scrap of sorrow, like a bird, lights on the heart.
I carry this in my body, seed
in an unswept corner, husk-encowled and seeming safe.
But they guard me, these small pains,
from growing sure
of myself and perhaps forgetting.

DIALOGUE

A friend says,
"I'm always practicing to be an old woman."
Another answers,
"I see myself young, maybe fourteen."

But when I lean to that mirror
a blackbird wing rises,
dark, flashing red at the shoulder,

and no woman is there
to pin flowers over the place
where her left breast lifts, falls.

TO DRINK

I want to gather your darkness
in my hands, to cup it like water
and drink.
I want this in the same way
as I want to touch your cheek—
it is the same—
the way a moth will come
to the bedroom window in late September,
beating and beating its wings against cold glass;
the way a horse will lower
its long head to water, and drink,
and pause to lift its head and look,
and drink again,
taking everything in with the water,
everything.

HEAT

My mare, when she was in heat,
would travel the fenceline for hours,
wearing the impatience
in her feet into the ground.

Not a stallion for miles, I'd assure her,
give it up.

She'd widen her nostrils,
sieve the wind for news, be moving again,
her underbelly darkening with sweat,
then stop at the gate a moment, wait
to see what I might do.
Oh, I knew
how it was for her, easily
recognized myself in that wide lust:
came to stand in the pasture
just to see it played.
Offered a hand, a bucket of grain,
a minute's distraction from passion
the most I gave.

Then she'd return to what burned her:
the fence, the fence,
so hoping I might see, might let her free.
I'd envy her then,
to be so restlessly sure
of heat, and need, and what it takes
to feed the wanting that we are—

Only a gap to open
the width of a mare,
the rest would take care of itself,
surely, surely I knew that,

who had the power of bucket
and bridle—
she would beseech me, sidle up,
be gone, as life is short.
But desire, desire is long.

TONIGHT THE INCALCULABLE STARS

Tonight the incalculable stars
have me thinking of
Catullus and his Lesbia,
who began counting once
and could not stop
until every schoolchild's tongue
pronounced their kisses
interminable,
stumbling through memorized passion
past ancient, jealous crones—
the old arithmetic of love,
got down by heart,
the hard way,
in a foreign tongue, too young.

There are names for what binds us:
strong forces, weak forces.
Look around, you can see them:
the skin that forms in a half-empty cup,
nails rusting into the places they join,
joints dovetailed on their own weight.
The way things stay so solidly
wherever they've been set down—
and gravity, scientists say, is weak.

And see how the flesh grows back
across a wound, with a great vehemence,
more strong
than the simple, untested surface before.
There's a name for it on horses,
when it comes back darker and raised: proud flesh,

as all flesh
is proud of its wounds, wears them
as honors given out after battle,
small triumphs pinned to the chest—

And when two people have loved each other
see how it is like a
scar between their bodies,
stronger, darker, and proud;
how the black cord makes of them a single fabric
that nothing can mend or tear.

NOVEMBER, REMEMBERING VOLTAIRE

In the evenings
I scrape my fingernails clean,
hunt through old catalogues for new seed,
oil workboots and shears.
This garden is no metaphor—
more a task that swallows you into itself,
earth using, as always, everything it can.
I lend myself to unpromising winter dirt
with leaf-mold and bulb,
plant into the oncoming cold.
Not that I ever thought
the philosopher meant to be taken literally,
but with no invented God overhead,
I conjure a stubborn faith in rotting
that ripens into soil,
in an old corm that rises steadily each spring:
not symbols, but reassurances,
like a mother's voice at bedtime reading a long-familiar book,
the known words barely listened to,
but joining, for all the nights of a life,
each world to the next.

EVENING, LATE FALL

It is not this world, then, to blame, with its red
and blue stars, yellow pears, green apples
that carry a scent which can move you to tears.
The others are not unlike this—
the women stand over sinks with their sleeves pushed back,
thin oxen lean into their yokes,
snow falls with impossible lightness in spring.
How do we bear it, then, to guess sometimes
at their lives across the dark?
How they sing as they run cotton towels across porcelain plates?
How they are innocent?

OSIRIS

They may tell you the god is broken
into a higher life,
but it isn't true:
the one who comes back remains,
even riveted, even pieced-
together in spring,
an always-broken god.
The knots survive in his body,
the clenched-grain scars.
And the iced, winter ponds are real:
the children, skating lightly there,
feel a secret shiver
as they cross the blue places
of darkness rising-to-meet,
where the other face of the god
is looking up.

Some questions cannot be answered.
They become familiar weights in the hand,
round stones pulled from the pocket,
unyielding and cool.
Your fingers travel their surfaces,
lose themselves finally
in the braille of the durable world.
Look out of any window, it's the same—
the yellow leaves, the wintering light.
A truck passes, piled deep in cut wood.
A woman, in a red wool coat,
sees you watching and quickly looks away.

JUSTICE WITHOUT PASSION

My neighbor's son, learning piano,
moves his fingers through the passages
a single note at a time, each lasting an equal interval,
each of them loud, distinct,
deliberate as a camel's walk through sand.
For him now, all is dispassion, a simple putting in place;
and so, giving equal weight to each mark in his folded-back book,
bending his head towards the difficult task,
he is like a soldier or a saint: blank-faced, and given wholly
to an obedience he does not need to understand.
He is even-handed, I think to myself,
and so, just. But in what we think of as music
there is no justice, nor in the evasive beauty of this boy,
glimpsed through his window across the lawn,
nor in what he will become, years from now, whatever he will become.
For now though, it is the same to him:
right note or wrong, he plays only for playing's sake
through the late afternoon, through stumbling and error,
through children's songs, Brahms, long-rehearsed, steady progressions
as he learns the ancient laws—that human action is judgment,
each note struggling with the rest.
That justice lacking passion fails, betrays.

On a quiet morning in autumn
I read the ledgers of a war,
as one can any day—
any list biased, dishonest, incomplete,
and still the numbers are kept.
It is true, the papyrus wears thin
after forty centuries.

For the winter garden
roses are pruned and carefully tied,
earth banked up over the roots.
What if after *Antigone*, the moment of catharsis,
we quarrel in the car going home?
If compassion cannot cure us?
What if we fail?

I look at my hands, my fingernails
still black with chosen labors.
I know that tomorrow I will go out again to mulch,
to bind, to clip, and that no order imposed
is free of guilt.
The line from a Greek chorus:
"Sing Sorrow, Sorrow, but Good win out in the end."
But who is measuring, what heart would choose this tune?

ON READING BRECHT

A child packs snow around a bit of stone
and throws it at his brother.
Each recalls this all his life,
the one who threw, and the one who cried out in surprise.
And whatever there is of love between them includes it.

So too, these words of Brecht's,
who could not forget
what man does to man in the name of art
or country, yet pressed these poems hard,
and threw.

Demosthenes, a wise man, filled his mouth
with pebbles before speaking,
and a stream which has run ten feet over rocks
is clear, they say, and safe to drink;
yet still we forget what is owed our failures—
blessings, to praise the stumbled on stone.
And forget what we once knew, how to properly greet
old enemies, for whose sake we practice and parry,
become strong:
with singing and banners, with gladness.

A STORY

A woman tells me
the story of a small wild bird,
beautiful on her windowsill, dead three days.
How her daughter came suddenly running,
"It's moving, Mommy, he's alive."
And when she went, it was.
The emerald wing-feathers
stirred, the throat
seemed to beat again with pulse.
Closer then, she saw how the true life lifted
under the wings. Turned her face
so her daughter would not see, though she would see.

CHILDHOOD, HORSES, RAIN

Again rain:
and the world like a fish held
under running water while the knife-blade
smooths the skin of scales.
Its twin eyes open, watching
not-death, not-life.
We shed our wild selves like this,
fearlessly, as water sheds its smoothness under wind,
and the image breaks, the white house, the apple trees,
the horses quivering with late summer flies as they graze,
the hundred wings brushing the lake of their backs.
Or the dog, who, seeing I will not open the door,
lies down at last to sleep: how, in her dream,
she chases down birds and barks softly.
How later the door will open, and she
in all her black and white ecstasy will burst through
to the scent of damp earth, return shaking rain from her
like seeds to the kitchen floor.
It is late and the dishes are finished, put away.
I towel her dry, she offers her feet up easily, as a horse
from long practice eases the farrier's work—
stands patiently at the hiss of hot iron dipped briefly
into a pail, cooled now and shaped to this one
curve of hoof, pared not quite to the quick;
and the swift blows with their stopped-bell ring.
As we learn to stand, for this world.

AUTUMN QUINCE

How sad they are,
the promises we never return to.
They stay in the mouth,
roughen the tongue, lead lives of their own.
Houses built for another to live in;
a succession of milk bottles brought to the door
every morning and taken inside.

And which piece is real?
The music in the composer's ear
or the lapsed one the orchestra plays?
The world is a blurred version of itself—
marred, lovely, and flawed.
It is enough.

FROM

The October Palace

(1994)

THE KINGDOM

At times
the heart
stands back
and looks at the body,
looks at the mind,
as a lion
quietly looks
at the not-quite-itself,
not-quite-another,
moving of shadows and grass.

Wary, but with interest,
considers its kingdom.

Then seeing
all that will be,
heart once again enters—
enters hunger, enters sorrow,
enters finally losing it all.
To know, if nothing else,
what it once owned.

EACH STEP

Nowhere on this earth
is it not a place where the lovers
turn lightly in sleep in each others' arms,
the blue pastures of dusk flowing gladly
into the dawn.

Nowhere that is not reached by the scent
of good bread
through an open window,
by the flash of fish in the flashing of summer streams,
or the trees unfolding their praises—
apricots, pears—of the winter-chill nights.

Briefly, briefly, we see it, and forget.
As if the spell were too powerful to hold on the tongue,
as if we preferred the weight to the prize—

Like a horse
that carries on his own back
the sacks of oats he will need, unsuspecting,
looking always ahead,
over the mountains, to where sweet springs lie.

He remembers this much from his youth,
the taste of things, cold and pure—

while the water-sound sings on and on, unlistened to,
in his ears;
while each step is nothing less than the glistening
river-body reentering home.

That winter we took turns stepping into
the barely started mornings to turn ignitions
until they caught, complaining roughly
of the cold, then ran
back to finish our coffee, cereal, toast,
while, chokes pulled full out,
exhaust poured white across the glass
that kept us warm.
We'd named them: Big Mama Tomato, Snooze.
Each was our first, as we
were each other's first, in the farmhouse
for rent for the first time
in forty years surrounded by soybeans.
We'd whited-over the pink room the son
had painted when he returned crazed with Vietnam.
We'd made the man come back for the thin black lab
left chained in the yard.
The thirteen cats stayed, soon more, all wild.
Our own would come to the window by way of
a three-story oak and moss-shingled porch roof,
to mew us awake and them in every day:
Kesey & Mountain Girl, scrawling their signatures
snow-mornings on the quilt.
We nailed planks from the old barns onto the walls
by our bed, scraped a dozen layers of peeling paper
from the next room—the older they got,
the more lovely. That one we made cheerful yellow,
where I wrote the wildly sad poems of the very young.
When we got to the farm you took a tractor, I loaded
my van with sacks of produce & drove off.
Kip supervised us all: the Peace Corps vet, the kids
just out of school. Picking his peaches that summer
the best work I've done, the closest to Paradise
I've seen, ladder-propped in his trees.
All sold now, gone, his farm, the one we lived at,
the groundfall cider, the cars.

Us too, of course, long shaken free, though
I still cook bluefish the way you taught me, and carrots.
I thought I would love you forever—and, a little, I may,
in the way I still move towards a crate, knees bent,
or reach for a man: as one might stretch
for the three or four fruits that lie in the sun at the top
of the tree; too ripe for any moment but this,
they open their skin at first touch, yielding sweetness,
sweetness and heat, and in me, each time since,
the answering yes.

THE GROUNDFALL PEAR

It is the one he chooses,
yellow, plump, a little bruised
on one side from falling.
That place he takes first.

PERCOLATION

In this rain that keeps us inside,
the frog,
wisest of creatures
to whom all things come,
is happy, rasping out of himself
the tuneless anthem of Frog.
Further off and more like ourselves,
the cows are raising a huddling protest,
a rag-tag crowd, that can't get its chanting in time.
Now the crickets,
seeming to welcome the early-come twilight,
come in—of all orchestras, the most plaintive.
Still, in this rain soft as fog
that can only be known to be rain by the windows' streaming,
surely all Being at bottom is happy:
soaked to the bone, sopped at the root,
fenny, seeped through, yielding as coffee grounds
yield to their percolation, blushing, completely seduced,
assenting as they give in to the downrushing water,
the murmur of falling, the fluvial, purling wash
of all the ways matter loves matter,
riding its gravity down, into the body,
rising through cell-strands of xylem, leaflet and lung-flower,
back into air.

I think it was from the animals
that St Francis learned
it is possible to cast oneself
on the earth's good mercy and live.
From the wolf who cast off
the deep fierceness of her first heart
and crept into the circle of sunlight
wagging her newly-shy tail
in full wariness and wolf-hunger,
and was fed, and lived; from the birds
who came fearless to him until he
had no choice but return that courage.
Even the least amoeba touched on all sides
by the opulent Other, even the baleened
plankton fully immersed in their fate—
for what else might happiness be
than to be porous, opened, rinsed through
by the beings and things?
Nor could he forget those other companions,
the shifting, ethereal, shapeless:
Hopelessness, Desperateness, Loneliness,
even the fire-tongued Anger—
for they too waited with the patient Lion,
the glossy Rooster, the drowsy Mule, to step
out of the trees' protection and come in.

THE LOVE OF AGED HORSES

Because I know tomorrow
his faithful gelding heart will be broken
when the spotted mare is trailered and driven away,
I come today to take him for a gallop on Diaz Ridge.

Returning, he will whinny for his love.
Ancient, spavined,
her white parts red with hill-dust,
her red parts whitened with the same, she never answers.

But today, when I turn him loose at the bent gate
with the taste of chewed oat on his tongue
and the saddle-sweat rinsed off with water,
I know he will canter, however tired,
whinnying wildly up the ridge's near side,
and I know he will find her.

He will be filled with the sureness of horses
whose bellies are grain-filled,
whose long-ribbed loneliness
can be scratched into no-longer-lonely.

His long teeth on her withers,
her rough-coated spots will grow damp and wild.
Her long teeth on his withers,
his oiled-teakwood smoothness will grow damp and wild.
Their shadows' chiasmus will fleck and fill with flies,
the eight marks of their fortune stamp and then cancel the earth.
From ear-flick to tail-switch, they stand in one body.
No luck is as boundless as theirs.

INSPIRATION

Think of those Chinese monks' tales:
years of struggling
in the zendo, then the clink,
while sweeping up, of stone on stone...
It's Emily's wisdom: Truth in Circuit lies.
Or see Grant's *Common Birds and How to Know Them*
(New York: Scribner's, 1901):
"The approach must be by detour,
advantage taken of rock, tree, mound, and brush,
but if without success this way, use artifice,
throw off all stealth's appearance, watchfulness,
look guileless, a loiterer, purposeless,
stroll on (not too directly toward the bird),
avoiding any gaze too steadfast;
or failing still in this, give voice to sundry whistles,
chirp: your quarry may stay on to answer."
More briefly, try; but stymied, give it up, do something else.
Leave the untrappable thought, go walking,
ideas buzz the air like flies. Return to work,
a fox trots by—not Hughes's sharp-stinking thought-fox
but quite real, outside the window,
with cream-dipped tail and red-fire legs doused watery brown.
Emerges from the wood's dark margin, stopping all thinking,
and briefly squats (not fox, but vixen), then moves along
and out of sight. "Enlightenment," wrote one master,
"is an accident, though certain efforts make you accident-prone."
The rest slants fox-like, in and out of stones.

HISTORY AS THE PAINTER BONNARD

Because nothing is ever finished
the painter would shuffle, *bonnarding*,
into galleries, museums, even the homes of his patrons,
with hidden palette and brush:
overscribble drapery and table with milk jug or fattened pear,
the clabbered, ripening colors of second sight.

Though he knew with time the pentimenti rise—
half-visible, half-brine-swept fish, their plunged shapes
pocking the mind—toward the end, only revision mattered:
to look again, more deeply, harder, clearer,
the one redemption granted us to ask.

This, we say, is what we meant to say. This. This.
—as the kiss, the sorrowful murmur,
may cover a child's bruises, if not retract the blow.
While a woman in Prague asks softly, in good English
for the camera, "But who will give us back these twenty years?"

Ah love, o history, forgive
the squandered light and flung-down rags of chances,
old choices drifted terribly awry.
And world, self-portrait never right, receive this gift—
shuffling, spattered, stubborn,
something nameless opens in the heart: to touch
with soft-bent sable, ground-earth pigment, seed-clear oil,
the rounding, bright-fleshed present, if not the past.

The kissed child puts his hand at last back into his mother's,
though it is not the same;
her fine face neither right nor wrong, only thoroughly his.

(Velvet Revolutions, November–December, 1989)

NARCISSUS: TEL AVIV, BAGHDAD, CALIFORNIA, FEBRUARY 1991

And then the precise
opening everywhere of the flowers,
which live after all in their own time.
It seemed they were oblivious but they were not,
they included it all, the nameless explosions
and the oil fires in every cell, the white petals
like mirrors opening in a slow-motion coming-apart
and the stems, the stems rising like green-flaring missiles,
like smoke, like the small sounds shaken
from those who were beaten—like dust from a carpet—
into the wind and the spring-scented rain.
They opened because it was time and they had no choice,
as the children were born in that time and that place
and became what they would without choice, or with only
a little choice, perhaps, for the lucky, the foolish or brave.
But precise and in fact wholly peaceful the flowers opened,
and precise and peaceful the earth: opened because it was asked.
Again and again it was asked and earth opened,
flowered and fell, because what was falling had asked
and could not be refused, as the seabirds that ask the green surface
to open are not refused but are instantly welcomed,
that they may enter and eat—
As soon refuse, battered and soaking, the dark mahogany rain.

THE WEDDING

Nothing is lost, nothing created: everything is transformed.

—Antoine-Laurent Lavoisier, *Elements of Chemistry*, 1789

The high windows stream with fish,
the gold luck of carp,
the tiny silver luck of minnows,
while the earth gives back her buried wealth
of skunks and star-crossed badgers:
pure stripes of seeing unfurl themselves
out of moonlight, and the dark bodies
follow as closely as boat follows sail
and know no harm will come to them in their wholeness.
All beings rise, uncaught, for this beginning.
Cousin Death joins a table at the wedding,
the white cloth gleams, the waiting plates,
all are made welcome.
Mother War smooths the silk of her dress,
she feels young and will dance again, after years,
with her husband, Pity.
Still the guests are arriving, carrying gifts:
small appliances, vases, a thick set of towels,
lamps of heaviest brass.
They say each other's names, Charity, Hope, and ask
of nieces and nephews off to school.
A rabbit edges near, outside the glass.
On the river a barge floats softly, its tugs at slack;
night herons and pelicans preen, an iron bell flames
with the slow ringing fire of rust and the barge imperceptibly
lowers. Imagine nothing created, what it might look like,
try to envision such peace.
Now see the dark-shelled flowers of thought unmade,
the petals of Little Boy unassembled,
the plague-poxed donkeys unflung over city walls, the dead
undead, the survivors unlonely. Or think of a world
in which nothing is lost, its heaped paintings,

the studded statues keeping their jewels.
Now see this very world, where all is transformed,
quick as a child who cries and then laughs in her crying—
now ingot, now blossoming ash,
now table, now suckling lamb on that table.
How each thing meets the other as itself, the luminous changing
mirror of itself: mercuric oxide tipped from flask to flask,
first two, then one, wedded for life in that vow.

A PLENITUDE

Even from a book of aging plates
these frescoes' intricate traceries
dazzle the eye
with their crazed-china 14th-century glaze:
in gold walls, gold vines
flicker and rise in intertwining diamonds,
in red bedding, damask blooms—
Each swath of floor or cloth
a plenitude that binds,
each peak-roofed canopy
a worked geometry of laddered tiles
or stones whose almost-symmetry is repetition
as in nature, invented always new.
These storied rooms seem not so much
built up by plan as breathed,
until at times they seem to break
as if from sheer exuberance to dapplings
seeded and selfless as animal pelts
or roots whose autumn pattern nets a hill
against the rain's entreating beat to join in falling.
Other times, though,
they seem delicately revealed,
as if some smooth and outer rind had been peeled back
to show the web of "'and' and 'and'," as Bishop wrote,
that is the world.
But there is the story, too,
of a young painter meeting the envoy of a Pope.
Asked for a work by which his art
could be weighed against others', he dipped his stylus—
with great courtesy, according to Vasari—
in red ink, and drew a single, perfect O.
Shocked, the messenger asked, "Will this be all?"
Giotto (whose deerfly his teacher had tried in vain
to brush from a painting) replied,
"It is enough and more."

THE DOOR

A note waterfalls steadily
through us,
just below hearing.

Or this early light
streaming through dusty glass:
what enters, enters like that,
unstoppable gift.

And yet there is also the other,
the breath-space held between any call
and its answer—

In the querying
first scuff of footstep,
the wood-owls' repeating,
the two-counting heart:

A little sabbath,
minnow whose brightness silvers past time.

The rest-note,
unwritten,
hinged between worlds,
that precedes change and allows it.

FLOOR

The nails, once inset, rise to the surface—
or, more truly perhaps, over years
the boards sink down to meet what holds them.
Worn, yes, but not worn through:
the visible work reveals itself in iron,
to be pounded down again, for what we've declared
the beautiful to be.

"PERCEPTIBILITY IS A KIND OF ATTENTIVENESS"

—Novalis

It is not enough
to see only the beauty,
this light
that pools aluminum
in the winter branches of apple—
it is only a sign
of the tree looking out
from the tree,
of the light looking
back at the light,
the long-celled attention.
The leaves too,
and the fruit, distract
in their sweetness and rustling.
As snow distracts,
covering the tree's looking out
with its own,
and the fragrance of blossoms.
Only stripped
of its multiple selves,
its many fabrics of loveliness,
does the tree's eye
step into a form
we can see with our own,
the black roots twisting down
from the heart,
ours equally whorled,
equally silent,
a flood-swept corridor keeping
no vision but life's—
A mirror looks into a mirror,
colorless, plain,
what flows between them
passes like water through a net.

A dragon-palace, but what dragon?
Its flowing scales of emerald,
emerald water;
its roaring rush,
tide-rush of water;
the treasure—oh even the treasure—
treasure of water.

THIS LOVE

Most lovely of the things I loved and lose: the sunlight;
next, bright stars, the moon,
ripe gourds, the fruit of apple trees, the pears.

—Praxilla (*fl.* 440 BCE)

A lucky woman,
Praxilla, to have tasted
the cucumber missed more severely than gold.
And lucky, whoever learns there is only one loss,
the bracelets glinting heavy and warm on the wrist,
fastened there for the first time
by a lover's hand,
and the lizard-cool fruit growing outside the door,
cobbled and rivered with all the green waters of earth.
Exiles, too, must know something
of how it will be, the ones who say not "I miss Paris"
but "Paris is missing me."
For it is the other which stays, we who depart,
and any piece of it, even the smallest, would more than suffice.
As lifting a single silk thread, the whole cloth must come,
if the silk is strong.
And this love we bear things—
their coarse hide, the blown chaff of their scent—
this love is strong.

But what if the world's
strict questions were not this
unanswerable yellow, that rampant red,
or the black-hearted, pried-open blue?
If the disciplined welter
were not heady with white-scented bloom?
Would love bend like the tulips then
from its quick-flying carriage?
Would tenderness wring the heart still
of its burdens, leaving only the dark-salted
circles on stone-colored ground?
It is the way humans know—
through the earth, through the things of the earth,
lips stained by what they have tasted,
the sweet sap-run, the tart-rinded fruit.
Leave to dogs and the angels
the music that lies beyond hearing.
Though the infinite palace is infinite, it is precise.

A SWEETENING ALL AROUND ME AS IT FALLS

Even generous August,
only a child's scribblings
on thick black paper, in smudgeable chalk—
even the ripening tomatoes, even the roses,
blowsy, loosing their fragrance of black tea.
A winter light held this morning's apples
as they fell, sweet, streaked by one touch
of the careless brush, appling to earth.
The seeds so deep inside they carry that cold.
Is this why some choose solitude, to rise
that small bit further, unencumbered by love of earth,
as the branches, lighter, kite now a little higher
on gold air? But the apples love earth and falling,
lose themselves in it as much as they can at first touch
and then, with time and rain, at last completely:
to be that bone-like One that shines unleafed in winter rain,
all black and glazed with not the pendant gold of
necklaced summer but the ice-color mirroring starlight
when the earth is empty and dark and knows nothing of apples.
Seed-black of the paper, seed-black of the waiting heart—
December's shine, austere and fragile, carves the visible tree.
But today, cut deep in last plums, in yellow pears,
in second flush of roses, in the warmth of an hour, now late,
as drunk on heat as the girl who long ago vanished into green trees,
fold that loneliness, one moment, two, love, back into your arms.

LEAVING THE OCTOBER PALACE

In ancient Japan, *to travel*
meant always away—
toward the capital, one spoke only of return.
As these falling needles and leaves speak of return,
their long labors of green tired finally into gold,
the desire that remembered them into place
prepared at last to let go.
Though not for want of faithfulness—
all that once followed the sun still follows it now,
as it turns away.
The courtiers assemble their carriages, fold up their robes.
By daybreak, the soundless mountains bow under snow.

AUTUMN

Again the wind
flakes gold-leaf from the trees
and the painting darkens—
as if a thousand penitents
kissed an icon
till it thinned
back to bare wood,
without diminishment.

Ripeness
is what falls away
with ease.
Not only the heavy apple,
the pear,
but also the dried brown strands
of autumn iris from their corm.

To let your body
love this world
that gave itself to your care
in all of its ripeness,
with ease,
and will take itself from you
in equal ripeness and ease,
is also harvest.

And however sharply
you are tested—
this sorrow, that great love—
it too will leave on that clean knife.

THE WEIGHING

The heart's reasons
seen clearly,
even the hardest
will carry
its whip-marks and sadness
and must be forgiven.

As the drought-starved
eland forgives
the drought-starved lion
who finally takes her,
enters willingly then
the life she cannot refuse,
and is lion, is fed,
and does not remember the other.

So few grains of happiness
measured against all the dark
and still the scales balance.

The world asks of us
only the strength we have and we give it.
Then it asks more, and we give it.

THE GODS ARE NOT LARGE

But perhaps
the heart
does not want
to be understood.
Your shadow
falls on its pond
and the small fish
hurry away.
They have
their own lives,
not yours,
which they love.

And if to you
it is anger,
bewilderment,
grief,
to them
it is simply life:
their mouths
open and close,
their gills,
they are fed,
they breathe.

The gods
are not large,
outside us.
They are the fish,
going on
with their own concerns.

THE HEART AS ORIGAMI

Each one has its shape.
For love, two sleeping ducks.
For selfless courage, the war horse.
For fear of death, the daylily's one-day flower.
More and more creased each year, worn paper thin,
and still it longs for them all.
Not one of the lives of this world the heart does not choose.

MEETING THE LIGHT COMPLETELY

Even the long-beloved
was once
an unrecognized stranger.

Just so,
the chipped lip
of a blue-glazed cup,
blown field
of a yellow curtain,
might also,
flooding and falling,
ruin your heart.

A table painted with roses.
An empty clothesline.

Each time,
the found world surprises—
that is its nature.

And then
what is said by all lovers:
"What fools we were, not to have seen."

WITHIN THIS TREE

Within this tree
another tree
inhabits the same body;
within this stone
another stone rests,
its many shades of gray
the same,
its identical
surface and weight.
And within my body,
another body,
whose history, waiting,
sings: *there is no other body*,
it sings,
there is no other world.

THE TASK

It is a simple garment, this slipped-on world.
We wake into it daily—open eyes, braid hair—
a robe unfurled
in rose-silk flowering, then laid bare.

And yes, it is a simple enough task
we've taken on,
though also vast:
from dusk to dawn,

from dawn to dusk, to praise,
and not be blinded by the praising.
To lie like a cat in the sun,
fur fully blazing,

and dream the mouse;
and to keep too the mouse's patient, waking watch
within the deep rooms of the house,
where the leaf-flocked

sunlight never reaches, but the earth still blooms.

EMPEDOCLES' PHYSICS

In all its parts the deep foul valley trembled so
I thought the universe felt love, which some believe
Has many times returned the world to chaos; here below
And elsewhere in that moment, the ancient cliffsides tumbled.

—*Inferno*, Canto XII

"Aversion carves the self."
—A Vedic teaching too, though here
it is Empedocles who wrote
that Hate creates our fractal'd world,
which Love would have a single, formless sphere.
An example: enemy soldiers, late
in 1914, carolled each other across the fields.
Could not, next dawn, take up their former places.
Such is the chaos that affection yields.

When did we cut the long-compounded verbs
into their separate nouns,
the worm's life from the bird's?
Must it be loneliness crowns all things
that live? Packed fat of the sea-lion,
fox blood splashing the brush like early sun—
why give them to our wars to be undone?
But if in truth Love's perfect One were
Dante's sheered disorder, the known world tumbled?
If the longing and stumble of self were made of sin?
Choose Hate, to stay faceted then
in the many and season-stung minds, the battered salmonskin
peeling its sky's flung rind, the blossoming strife.
Choose the cell's dividing, life into life,
the too-bright stream. Choose beauty loved—
how loved—within division's light.

THE STONE OF HEAVEN

Here, where the rivers dredge up
the very stone of Heaven, we name its colors—
muttonfat jade, kingfisher jade, jade of appleskin green.

And here, in the glittering
hues of the Flemish Masters, we sample their wine;
rest in their windows' sun-warmth,
cross with pleasure their scrubbed tile floors.
Everywhere the details leap like fish—bright shards
of water out of water, facet-cut, swift-moving
on the myriad bones.

Any woodthrush shows it: he sings,
not to fill the world, but because he is filled.

But the world does not fill with us,
it spills and spills, whirs with owl-wings,
rises, sets, stuns us with planet-rings, stars.
A carnival tent, a fluttering of banners.

O baker of yeast-scented loaves,
sword dancer,
seamstress, weaver of shattering glass,
O whirler of winds, boat-swallower,
germinant seed,
O seasons that sing in our ears in the shape of O—
we name your colors muttonfat, kingfisher, jade,
we name your colors anthracite, orca, growth-tip of pine,
we name them arpeggio, pond,
we name them flickering helix within the cell, burning coal tunnel,
    blossom of salt,
we name them roof flashing copper, frost-scent at morning, smoke-singe
    of pearl,
from black-flowering to light-flowering we name them,

from barest conception, the almost not thought of, to heaviest matter,
    we name them,
from glacier-lit blue to the gold of iguana we name them,
and naming, begin to see,
and seeing, begin to assemble the plain stones of earth.

The Lives of the Heart

SECRETIVE HEART

—What's this? This is an old toolshed.
No, this is a great past love

—Yehuda Amichai

Heart falters, stops
before a Chinese cauldron
still good for boiling water.

It is one of a dozen or more,
it is merely iron,
it is merely old,
there is much else to see.

The few raised marks
on its belly
are useful to almost no one.

Heart looks at it a long time.
What do you see? I ask again,
but it does not answer.

MULE HEART

On the days when the rest
have failed you,
let this much be yours—
flies, dust, an unnameable odor,
the two waiting baskets:
one for the lemons and passion,
the other for all you have lost.
Both empty,
it will come to your shoulder,
breathe slowly against your bare arm.
If you offer it hay, it will eat.
Offered nothing,
it will stand as long as you ask.
The little bells of the bridle will hang
beside you quietly,
in the heat and the tree's thin shade.
Do not let its sparse mane deceive you,
or the way the left ear swivels into dream.
This too is a gift of the gods,
calm and complete.

SALT HEART

I was tired,
half sleeping in the sun.
A single bee
delved the lavender nearby,
and beyond the fence,
a trowel's shoulder knocked a white stone.
Soon, the ringing stopped.
And from somewhere,
a quiet voice said the one word.
Surely a command,
though it seemed more a question,
a wondering perhaps—"What about joy?"
So long it had been forgotten,
even the thought raised surprise.
But however briefly, there,
in the untuned devotions of bee
and the lavender fragrance,
the murmur of better and worse was unimportant.
From next door, the sound of raking,
and neither courage nor cowardice mattered.
Failure—uncountable failure—did not matter.
Soon enough that gate swung closed,
the world turned back to heart-salt
of wanting, heart-salts of will and grief.
My friend would continue dying, at last
only exhausted, even his wrists thinned with pain.
The river Suffering would take what it
wished of him, then go. And I would stay
and drink on, as the living do, until the rest
would enter into that water—the lavender swept in,
the bee, the swallowed labors of my neighbor.
The ordinary moment swept in, whatever it drowsily holds.
I begin to believe the only sin is distance, refusal.
All others stemming from this. Then come.
Rivers, come. Irrevocable futures, come. Come even joy.
Even now, even here, and though it vanish like him.

ON THE BEACH

Uncountable tiny pebbles
of many colors.

Broken seashells mixed in with whole ones.

Sand dollars, shattered and whole,
the half-gone wing of a gull.

Changed glass
that is like the heart after much pain.
The empty shell of a crab.

A child moves alone in the gray
that is half fog, half wind-blown ocean.

She lifts one pebble, another,
into her pocket.
From time to time takes them out again and looks.

These few and only these. How many? Why?

The waves continue their work of breaking
then rounding the edges.

I would speak to her if I could,
but across the distance what would she hear?
Ocean and ocean. Cry of a fish.

Walk slowly now, small soul, by the edge
of the water. Choose carefully
all you are going to lose, though any of it would do.

HEART STARTING AND STOPPING IN THE LATE DARK

I cannot tell
if this night singing comes
from inside or outside the house,
though today a cricket walked
across my papers on the floor.
He made a little clicking sound
as he passed, from his strange knees,
or his feet on the paper.
He seemed to know where he wanted to get to.
When the dying Bonnard had his nephew
add the new yellow-gold to *Almond in Blossom*,
it was his signature he canceled for that other.
This late typing, starting and stopping,
is not so different from a cricket's walking
to the night's ear, I think—
if the night had an ear. Perhaps that is what
started him singing wherever he is,
startled by my insomnia into his one word,
which is filled, I think, with dignity,
which is filled, I think, with trust.
I would like to go, as at last Bonnard did,
all the way into the world of the living.
To sit there a while in the petals, altering nothing.

You must try,
the voice said, to become colder.
I understood at once.
It is like the bodies of gods: cast in bronze,
braced in stone. Only something heartless
could bear the full weight.

THE ADAMANTINE PERFECTION OF DESIRE

Nothing more strong
than to be helpless before desire.

No reason,
the simplified heart whispers,
the argument over,
only This.

No longer choosing anything but assent.

Its bowl scraped clean to the bottom,
the skull-bone cup no longer horrifies,
but, rimmed-in-silver, shines.

A spotted dog follows a bitch in heat.
Gray geese fly past us, crying.
The living cannot help but love the world.

STANDING DEER

As the house of a person
in age sometimes grows cluttered
with what is
too loved or too heavy to part with,
the heart may grow cluttered.
And still the house will be emptied,
and still the heart.

As the thoughts of a person
in age sometimes grow sparer,
like a great cleanness come into a room,
the soul may grow sparer;
one sparrow song carves it completely.
And still the room is full,
and still the heart.

Empty and filled,
like the curling half-light of morning,
in which everything is still possible and so why not.

Filled and empty,
like the curling half-light of evening,
in which everything now is finished and so why not.

Beloved, what can be, what was,
will be taken from us.
I have disappointed.
I am sorry. I knew no better.

A root seeks water.
Tenderness only breaks open the earth.
This morning, out the window,
three deer stood like a blessing, then vanished.

I was walking again
in the woods,
a yellow light
was sifting all I saw.

Willfully,
with a cold heart,
I took a stick,
lifted it to the opposite side
of the path.

There, I said to myself,
that's done now.
Brushing one hand against the other,
to clean them
of the tiny fragments of bark.

Take the used-up heart like a pebble
and throw it far out.

Soon there is nothing left.
Soon the last ripple exhausts itself
in the weeds.

Returning home, slice carrots, onions, celery.
Glaze them in oil before adding
the lentils, water, and herbs.

Then the roasted chestnuts, a little pepper, the salt.
Finish with goat cheese and parsley. Eat.
You may do this, I tell you, it is permitted.
Begin again the story of your life.

NOT-YET

Morning of buttered toast;
of coffee, sweetened, with milk.

Out the window,
snow-spruces step from their cobwebs.
Flurry of chickadees, feeding then gone.
A single cardinal stipples an empty branch—
one maple leaf lifted back.

I turn my blessings like photographs into the light;
over my shoulder the god of Not-Yet looks on:

Not-yet-dead, not-yet-lost, not-yet-taken.
Not-yet-shattered, not-yet-sectioned,
not-yet-strewn.

Ample litany, sparing nothing I hate or love:
Not-yet-silenced, not-yet-fractured, not-yet-

Not-yet-not.

I move my ear a little closer to that humming figure,
I ask him only to stay.

THREE FOXES BY THE EDGE OF
THE FIELD AT TWILIGHT

One ran,
her nose to the ground,
a rusty shadow
neither hunting nor playing.

One stood; sat; lay down; stood again.

One never moved,
except to turn her head a little as we walked.

Finally we drew too close,
and they vanished.
The woods took them back as if they had never been.

I wish I had thought to put my face to the grass.

But we kept walking,
speaking as strangers do when becoming friends.

There is more and more I tell no one,
strangers nor loves.
This slips into the heart
without hurry, as if it had never been.

And yet, among the trees, something has changed.

Something looks back from the trees,
and knows me for who I am.

LEAF

Large as two hands together
still cupping rain,
yellow of amber stripped lightless,
scent of cold leather.
Nameless, one of ten thousand,
lifted without complaint or hope
to this painted table,
neither envelope nor letter.
Almost nothing. Yet before you,
words lie down in envy and silence,
switch their tails,
bury their damp, dark snouts between paws.

HOPE AND LOVE

All winter
the blue heron
slept among the horses.
I do not know
the custom of herons,
do not know
if the solitary habit
is their way,
or if he listened for
some missing one—
not knowing even
that was what he did—
in the blowing
sounds in the dark.
I know that
hope is the hardest
love we carry.
He slept
with his long neck
folded, like a letter
put away.

LATE PRAYER

Tenderness does not choose its own uses.
It goes out to everything equally,
circling rabbit and hawk.
Look: in the iron bucket,
a single nail, a single ruby—
all the heavens and hells.
They rattle in the heart and make one sound.

EACH HAPPINESS RINGED BY LIONS

Sometimes when
I take you into my body
I can almost see them—patient, circling.
Almost glimpse the moving shadow of the tail,
almost hear the hushed pad of retracted claws.
It is the moment—of this I am certain—
when they themselves are least sure.
It is the moment they could almost let us go free.

EACH MOMENT A WHITE BULL STEPS
SHINING INTO THE WORLD

If the gods bring to you
a strange and frightening creature,
accept the gift
as if it were one you had chosen.

Say the accustomed prayers,
oil the hooves well,
caress the small ears with praise.

Have the new halter of woven silver
embedded with jewels.
Spare no expense, pay what is asked,
when a gift arrives from the sea.

Treat it as you yourself
would be treated,
brought speechless and naked
into the court of a king.

And when the request finally comes,
do not hesitate even an instant—

Stroke the white throat,
the heavy, trembling dewlaps
you've come to believe were yours,
and plunge in the knife.

Not once
did you enter the pasture
without pause,
without yourself trembling.
That you came to love it, that was the gift.

Let the envious gods take back what they can.

ORANGE OIL IN DARKNESS

The useful part
of things is elegance—
in mathematics, bridges.

Even in hedges
of ripe persimmons
or mandarin oranges,

elegance solves
for the minimum possible,
then dissolves.

The art is what is extra:
a fragrance penciled in,
or long division's inescapable remainder.

Not quite unplanned for,
more the unexpected, impractical gift.
Not the figures traced

in the bridge's stanchions,
but the small
and lovely sounds they make in the wind.

Who drew that in?
Who could have?
For years now I've mistaken

art for beauty,
but it is not beauty.
Art lives in a plenitude more iron,

more empty, less demanding.
Art doesn't care,
except in moments of despair.

Those it lets pass, recognizing weakness.

THE SWEETNESS OF APPLES, OF FIGS

In Bellini's painting,
the usual angel
is not present,
only a man
opening his chest
to the world
of simple sheep
and goose and hare
in the strange light.
Book and skull,
the two wooden sandals,
lie forgotten
behind the open-lattice door.
Even his pin-pricked
hands, it seems, forgotten.
Again the holy striving
has given way
to ordinary joy.
It is mostly blues,
a little reddish-brown,
some green.

WINE GRAPES FOR BREAKFAST

Sweet
at first
on the tongue,
hours later
the red grapes
still sting,
as if trying
to tell me something—
what the hook
tells the fish
perhaps,
or the wand
or stick hears
before conductor
or mule driver
brings it down.

BEES

In every instant, two gates.
One opens to fragrant paradise, one to hell.
Mostly we go through neither.

Mostly we nod to our neighbor,
lean down to pick up the paper,
go back into the house.

But the faint cries—ecstasy? horror?
Or did you think it the sound
of distant bees,
making only the thick honey of this good life?

I want to give myself
utterly
as this maple
that burned and burned
for three days without stinting
and then in two more
dropped off every leaf;
as this lake that,
no matter what comes
to its green-blue depths,
both takes and returns it.
In the still heart,
that refuses nothing,
the world is twice-born—
two earths wheeling,
two heavens,
two egrets reaching
down into subtraction;
even the fish
for an instant doubled,
before it is gone.
I want the fish.
I want the losing it all
when it rains and I want
the returning transparence.
I want the place
by the edge-flowers where
the shallow sand is deceptive,
where whatever
steps in must plunge,
and I want that plunging.
I want the ones
who come in secret to drink
only in early darkness,
and I want the ones
who are swallowed.

I want the way
this water sees without eyes,
hears without ears,
shivers without will or fear
at the gentlest touch.
I want the way it
accepts the cold moonlight
and lets it pass,
the way it lets
all of it pass
without judgment or comment.
There is a lake,
Lalla Ded sang, no larger
than one seed of mustard,
that all things return to.
O heart, if you
will not, cannot, give me the lake,
then give me the song.

MILK

From time to time the placid
shrugs its shoulders—
earthquakes, for instance—

but still the world
depends
on placid things' resistance.

The fire requires
its trees,
the sea its hem of boulders,

the wind
without its halls
would howl in silence;

for everything that
flares up, something lowers
itself, digs in

for an existence
in the long haul, slows.
It may well be the placid knows

its worth. The cow whose
calf was taken
eats again—but do not guess

too quickly at the meaning
in the red hips' unbent squareness,
the large-jawed head

half-buried in the grass:
with each fly's weightless
bite, the thick skin shivers.

The placid, unlike us,
lives in the moment.
Something must.

Like chairs,
or painted dressers,
on an earth where loss

is so all present
that we drink it without thinking,
blue-white in its early morning glass.

JASMINE

"Almost the twenty-first century"—
how quickly the thought will grow dated,
even quaint.

Our hopes, our future,
will pass like the hopes and futures of others.

And all our anxieties and terrors,
nights of sleeplessness,
griefs,
will appear then as they truly are—

Stumbling, delirious bees in the tea scent of jasmine.

She is working now, in a room
not unlike this one,
the one where I write, or you read.
Her table is covered with paper.
The light of the lamp would be
tempered by a shade, where the bulb's
single harshness might dissolve,
but it is not, she has taken it off.
Her poems? I will never know them,
though they are the ones I most need.
Even the alphabet she writes in
I cannot decipher. Her chair—
Let us imagine whether it is leather
or canvas, vinyl or wicker. Let her
have a chair, her shadeless lamp,
the table. Let one or two she loves
be in the next room. Let the door
be closed, the sleeping ones healthy.
Let her have time, and silence,
enough paper to make mistakes and go on.

BLIND FATE WALKING ON ICE IN THE WOODS

The mildest slope of her guide dog's
shoulders
makes a difference. The yaw

of the wind in the harness
makes a difference.
Everything here is ice-clear,
even to her.

I balance on my eyes. The rest of us do—
vision's two canes
like a walker set down before us.

Now she is passing
close enough almost to kiss.

Cold scent of wool, of soup.

Her life.

If you looked into her face,
you would fall in an instant.

THE BEARDED WOMAN

Each time she noticed,
she had meant
to pluck the three black hairs,
but the days were short;
her fingers touched her chin
then forgot.
Thus fatigue grew curling into wisdom.

SPELL FOR INVITING-IN THE NEW SOUL

Shy one,
small donkey, come forward.
Let world be cradle.

Fish drifting, enter weight gladly.
Trust passage.

If suffering will chant you,
if terror,
in pine dark, deer breathing.
In sea-bench's sorrow gills salt-light.

Know owl-cries your forelock.

Know leaf-scent, know cities, know rivers,
know doorways stand open.
In ice-grip, know muskrat's strong swimming.
Let asking.

Let losing and breaking, let weather.
Let entrance entirely.
Desires bray sweet in the ladders of loudness.

Shy one, small donkey, trust hoof-fall.
Seeds wait to ride on your ankles,
five baskets
of apple sleep guardian.

The bridle placed heavy wears bell-sounds.
Agreeing come forward.

SPELL TO BE SAID BEFORE SLEEP

Each pot now hang bright
on the black peg;
grief, mend the owl's wing further.

Who will follow her singing
into the river, into the mountain?
Now it is one note, now two,
the moon hurried into the snow.

Shines back the breath of the mare.
Lucent,
dreaming the mountain of moment and moment,
black tail bless the dark.

Slender the bones
of the forelegs all night keeping watch,
stand over the one who is sleeping.
Stand over the owl.
Three times brush the tail of the darkness.

One stone in the bed of the River of Heaven
is the mare.
One is the owl. One is the singing.

Guard them, o earth, in your travels.

SPELL TO BE SAID UPON DEPARTURE

What was come here to do
having finished,
shelves of the water lie flat.

Copper the leaves of the doorsill,
yellow and falling.
Scarlet the bird that is singing.

Vanished the labor, here walls are.
Completed the asking.
Loosing the birds there is water.

Having eaten the pears.
Having eaten
the black figs, the white figs. Eaten the apples.

Table be strewn.
Table be strewn with stems,
table with peelings of grapefruit and pleasure.

Table be strewn with pleasure,
what was here to be done having finished.

THREE TIMES MY LIFE HAS OPENED

Three times my life has opened.
Once, into darkness and rain.
Once, into what the body carries at all times within it and starts
    to remember each time it enters the act of love.
Once, to the fire that holds all.
These three were not different.
You will recognize what I am saying or you will not.
But outside my window all day a maple has stepped from her leaves
    like a woman in love with winter, dropping the colored silks.
Neither are we different in what we know.
There is a door. It opens. Then it is closed. But a slip of light
    stays, like a scrap of unreadable paper left on the floor,
    or the one red leaf the snow releases in March.

Given Sugar, Given Salt

(2001)

THE ENVOY

One day in that room, a small rat.
Two days later, a snake.

Who, seeing me enter,
whipped the long stripe of his
body under the bed,
then curled like a docile house-pet.

I don't know how either came or left.
Later, the flashlight found nothing.

For a year I watched
as something—terror? happiness? grief?—
entered and then left my body.

Not knowing how it came in,
Not knowing how it went out.

It hung where words could not reach it.
It slept where light could not go.
Its scent was neither snake nor rat,
neither sensualist nor ascetic.

There are openings in our lives
of which we know nothing.

Through them
the belled herds travel at will,
long-legged and thirsty, covered with foreign dust.

RED BERRIES

Again the pyracantha berries redden in rain,
as if return were return.

It is not.

The familiar is not the thing it reminds of.
Today's *yes* is different from yesterday's *yes*.
Even *no*'s adamance alters.

From painting to painting,
century to century,
the tipped-over copper pot spills out different light;
the cut-open beeves,
their caged and muscled display,
are on one canvas radiant, pure; obscene on another.

In the end it is simple enough—

The woman of this morning's mirror
was a stranger
to the woman of last night's;
the passionate dreams of the one who slept
flit empty and thin
from the one who awakens.

One woman washes her face,
another picks up the boar-bristled hairbrush,
a third steps out of her slippers.
That each will die in the same bed means nothing to them.

Our one breath follows another like spotted horses, no two alike.

Black manes and white manes, they gallop.
Piebald and skewbald, eyes flashing sorrow, they too will pass.

APPLE

I woke and remembered
nothing of what I was dreaming.

The day grew light, then dark again—
In all its rich hours, what happened?

A few weeds pulled, a few cold flowers
carried inside for the vase.
A little reading. A little tidying and sweeping.

I had vowed to do nothing I did not wish
to do that day, and kept my promise.

Once, a certain hope came close
and then departed. Passed by me in its familiar
shawl, scented with iodine woodsmoke.

I did not speak to it, nor it to me.
Yet still the habit of warmth traveled
between us, like an apple shared by old friends—

One takes a bite, then the other.
They do this until it is gone.

A HAND

A hand is not four fingers and a thumb.

Nor is it palm and knuckles,
not ligaments or the fat's yellow pillow,
not tendons, star of the wristbone, meander of veins.

A hand is not the thick thatch of its lines
with their infinite dramas,
nor what it has written,
not on the page,
not on the ecstatic body.

Nor is the hand its meadows of holding, of shaping—
not sponge of rising yeast-bread,
not rotor pin's smoothness,
not ink.

The maple's green hands do not cup
the proliferant rain.
What empties itself falls into the place that is open.

A hand turned upward holds only a single, transparent question.

Unanswerable, humming like bees, it rises, swarms, departs.

HABIT

The shoes put on each time
left first, then right.

The morning potion's teaspoon
of sweetness stirred always
for seven circlings—no fewer, no more—
into the cracked blue cup.

Touching the pocket for wallet,
for keys,
before closing the door.

How did we come
to believe these small rituals' promise,
that we are today the selves we yesterday knew,
tomorrow will be?

How intimate and unthinking,
the way the toothbrush is shaken dry after use,
the part we wash first in the bath.

Which habits we learned from others
and which are ours alone we may never know.
Unbearable to acknowledge
how much they are themselves our fated life.

Open the traveling suitcase—

There the beloved red sweater,
bright tangle of necklace, earrings of amber.
Each confirming: I chose these, I.

But habit is different: it chooses.
And we, its good horse,
opening our mouths at even the sight of the bit.

REBUS

You work with what you are given,
the red clay of grief,
the black clay of stubbornness going on after.
Clay that tastes of care or carelessness,
clay that smells of the bottoms of rivers or dust.

Each thought is a life you have lived or failed to live,
each word is a dish you have eaten or left on the table.
There are honeys so bitter
no one would willingly choose to take them.
The clay takes them: honey of weariness, honey of vanity,
honey of cruelty, fear.

This rebus—slip and stubbornness,
bottom of river, my own consumed life—
when will I learn to read it
plainly, slowly, uncolored by hope or desire?
Not to understand it, only to see.

As water given sugar sweetens, given salt grows salty,
we become our choices.
Each *yes*, each *no* continues,
this one a ladder, that one an anvil or cup.

The ladder leans into its darkness.
The anvil leans into its silence.
The cup sits empty.

How can I enter this question the clay has asked?

WAKING THIS MORNING DREAMLESS
AFTER LONG SLEEP

But with this sentence:
"Use your failures for paper."
Meaning, I understood,
the backs of failed poems, but also my life.

Whose far side I begin now to enter—

A book imprinted without seeming reason,
each blank day bearing on its reverse, in random order,
the mad-set type of another.
December 12, 1960. April 4, 1981. 13th of August, 1974—

Certain words bleed through to the unwritten pages.
To call this memory offers no solace.

"Even in sleep, the heavy millstones turning."

I do not know where the words come from,
what the millstones,
where the turning may lead.

I, a woman forty-five, beginning to gray at the temples,
putting pages of ruined paper
into a basket, pulling them out again.

BOBCATS, BEETLES, OWLS

We stood in the dark outside a door
and talked in the scent of jasmine.

Three women standing at the foot of—what?
One mountain of three lifetimes' lucks and losses,
the other actual and breathing, above us in the dark.

The year's new leaves and grasses were resting all around us.
Somewhere above us, deer were sleeping.
Bobcats, beetles, owls, were sleeping.

We spoke of neither mountain.
We breathed in the scent of jasmine between words
whose meaning didn't matter.
Only the murmur mattered, going on.

It was night. Deer slept, and bobcats.
Our lives paused with us in the doorway, waiting.

GREAT POWERS ONCE RAGED THROUGH YOUR BODY

Great powers once raged
through your body, waking and sleeping.
What remains?

A few words, your own or others'.
A freshened affection for silence and rest;
but also for lightning and wind,
familiar to you now as your own coat or shoes.

They lie on the closet floor
in the scent of paint and pinewood,
as if you had picked them out for yourself,
as if you had carried them home.

"What could have happened, has happened."
The sentence repeats itself in your ear
as a pear repeats itself, each time a little altered,
on every branch of the tree.

Chair, table, dishcloth, bowl—
each thing under your hand or your eyes
you regard now as ally, as friend.

And yet this hard-won composure
feels already a little simple, a little meek—
like a painting
of yellow houses or fields, before
the narrow slashes of red have been riveted in.

THE CONTRACT

The woman who gave me the rosebush
reminds me:
"Cut it back hard."

The stems resist.

Thorns and weedy twig-thickets
catch on jacket sleeve, on gloves.
Core-wood splinters green under the shears.

Impossible to believe
that so little left will lead to fragrance.

Still, my hands move quickly,
adding their signature branch by branch,
agreeing to loss.

RED ONION, CHERRIES, BOILING POTATOES, MILK—

Here is a soul, accepting nothing.
Obstinate as a small child
refusing tapioca, peaches, toast.

The cheeks are streaked, but dry.
The mouth is firmly closed in both directions.

Ask, if you like,
if it is merely sulking, or holding out for better.
The soup grows cold in the question.
The ice cream pools in its dish.

Not this, is all it knows. Not this.
As certain cut flowers refuse to drink in the vase.

And the heart, from its great distance, watches, helpless.

THIS WAS ONCE A LOVE POEM

This was once a love poem,
before its haunches thickened, its breath grew short,
before it found itself sitting,
perplexed and a little embarrassed,
on the fender of a parked car,
while many people passed by without turning their heads.

It remembers itself dressing as if for a great engagement.
It remembers choosing these shoes,
this scarf or tie.

Once, it drank beer for breakfast,
drifted its feet
in a river side by side with the feet of another.

Once it pretended shyness, then grew truly shy,
dropping its head so the hair would fall forward,
so the eyes would not be seen.

It spoke with passion of history, of art.
It was lovely then, this poem.
Under its chin, no fold of skin softened.
Behind the knees, no pad of yellow fat.
What it knew in the morning it still believed at nightfall.
An unconjured confidence lifted its eyebrows, its cheeks.

The longing has not diminished.
Still it understands. It is time to consider a cat,
the cultivation of African violets or flowering cactus.

Yes, it decides:
many miniature cacti, in blue and red painted pots.

When it finds itself disquieted
by the pure and unfamiliar silence of its new life,
it will touch them—one, then another—
with a single finger outstretched like a tiny flame.

BUTTON

It likes both to enter and to leave,
actions it seems to feel as a kind of hide-and-seek.
It knows nothing of what the cloth believes
of its magus-like powers.

If fastening and unfastening are its nature,
it doesn't care about its nature.

It likes the caress of two fingers
against its slightly thickened edges.
It likes the scent and heat of the proximate body.
The exhilaration of the washing is its wild pleasure.

Amoralist, sensualist, dependent of cotton thread,
its sleep is curled like a cat to a patch of sun,
calico and round.

Its understanding is the understanding
of honey and jasmine, of letting what happens come.

A button envies no neighboring button,
no snap, no knot, no polyester-braided toggle.
It rests on its red-checked shirt in serene disregard.

It is its own story, completed.

Brevity and longevity mean nothing to a button carved of horn.

Nor do old dreams of passion disturb it,
though once it wandered the ten thousand grasses
with the musk-fragrance caught in its nostrils;
though once it followed—it did, I tell you—that wind for miles.

I haven't yet found the pronoun through which to touch it directly.
You may feel differently.
You may think you can simply reach through all the way
   with your hand, like petting the shoulder of an old dog, who, when
she can no longer stand, lies on her bed, watching her kingdom
   arriving and leaving, arriving and leaving, until at last
it only departs.
We want our lives and deaths to be like that—something formal, a
   kingdom. Filled with the sense of the manyness of existence. As the
   French say
"*Vous*" to that which cannot yet be made familiar.
They do this less and less these days, it seems.

"If you wish to move your reader,"
Chekhov wrote, "you must write more coldly."

Herakleitos recommended, "A dry soul is best."

And so at the center of many great works
is found a preserving dispassion,
like the vanishing point of quattrocento perspective,
or the tiny packets of desiccant enclosed
in a box of new shoes or seeds.

But still the vanishing point
is not the painting,
the silica is not the blossoming plant.

Chekhov, dying, read the timetables of trains.
To what more earthly thing could he have been faithful?—
Scent of rocking distances,
smoke of blue trees out the window,
hampers of bread, pickled cabbage, boiled meat.

Scent of the knowable journey.

Neither a person entirely broken
nor one entirely whole can speak.

In sorrow, pretend to be fearless. In happiness, tremble.

HAPPINESS IS HARDER

To read a book of poetry
from back to front,
there is the cure for certain kinds of sadness.

A person has only to choose.
What doesn't matter; just *that*—

This coffee. That dress.
"Here is the time I would like to arrive."
"Today, I will wash the windows."

Happiness is harder.

Consider the masters' description
of awakened existence, how seemingly simple:
Hungry, I eat; sleepy, I sleep.
Is this choosing completely, or not at all?

In either case, everything seems to conspire against it.

LIKE AN ANT CARRYING HER BITS OF LEAF OR SAND

Like an ant carrying her bits of leaf or sand,
the poem carries its words.
Moving one, then another, into place.

Something in an ant is sure where these morsels belong,
but the ant could not explain this.
Something in a poem is certain where its words belong,
but the poet could not explain this.

All day the ant obeys an inexplicable order.
All day the poet obeys an incomprehensible demand.

The world changes or does not change by these labors;
the geode peeled open gives off its cold scent or does not.
But that is no concern of the ant's, of the poem's.

The work of existence devours its own unfolding.
What dissolves will dissolve—
you, reader, and I, and all our quick angers and longings.
The potato's sugary hunger for growing larger.
The unblinking heat of the tiger.

No thimble of cloud or stone that will not vanish,
and still the rearrangements continue.

The ant's work belongs to the ant.
The poem carries love and terror, or it carries nothing.

PILLOW

Some pillows are made of down, feathers,
and striped cotton ticking,
some of wool or dried herb flowers,
others of thought.

The thought of a good sandwich
in the lunch bag for instance—
provolone slices and garden tomato,
a little dijon and mayonnaise—can be a pillow,

comforting as the memory of being,
for one moment,
not entirely embarrassed to be human.

Able, say, to meet the gaze
of a cow or a horse with eyes neither arrogant
nor lowered, to offer a carrot
not as propitiation or bribe but simple friendship.

Friendship can be simple,
like the pillow of a horseshoe's lucky curve
above a door where it's needed.

"Here," I said to my friend when he was dying.
"Here," he replied.

There was nothing more to ask of one another,
though we spoke a while longer,
words like river pebbles, some black, some white,
wrapped in a handkerchief's tied-together purse.

I could not eat them,
so I put them under my pillow that night,
and slept well,
without dismay or turning,
though he would continue dying, though I would live.

His look, those days: plain as water, undeterred
by the ongoing disassemblage.
A little greedy, but also ready, prepared.

Whatever came, he told me, would be his own luck.

We held hands a time,
then together let go that touch,
together turned to our separate tasks,

like the two hands
of a person arranging the blankets and pillow
just so before sleeping,
settling the one day in order to enter the next.

Say "death" and the whole room freezes—
even the couches stop moving,
even the lamps.
Like a squirrel suddenly aware it is being looked at.

Say the word continuously,
and things begin to go forward.
Your life takes on
the jerky texture of an old film strip.

Continue saying it,
hold it moment after moment inside the mouth,
it becomes another syllable.
A shopping mall swirls around the corpse of a beetle.

Death is voracious, it swallows all the living.
Life is voracious, it swallows all the dead.
Neither is ever satisfied, neither is ever filled,
each swallows and swallows the world.

The grip of life is as strong as the grip of death.

(but the vanished, the vanished beloved, o where?)

"NOTHING LASTS"

"Nothing lasts"—
how bitterly the thought attends each loss.

"Nothing lasts"—
a promise also of consolation.

Grief and hope
the skipping rope's two ends,
twin daughters of impatience.

One wears a dress of wool, the other cotton.

One night eating potatoes pan-fried,
the next night baked, two nights later, mashed.
A hummingbird drives at the evening fuchsia,
still sunlit this far north.
Because I have seen this before, I think
my hummingbird is drinking. And later, *my four-point buck*—
who also likes the red flowers.
If the hummingbird is thinking, *my pendant fuchsia*,
my watching human, I will not know it.
Then in broad evening brightness the raccoon
races its shadow across the mown grass.
Not *my raccoon*—it's Eleanor and Richard's, next door.
Each of us racing with him, making our own
for a little while, as travelers do, what is no one's.
Every third morning here I wake from another nightmare,
and still I find myself thinking: *paradise, bliss.*

ALL EVENING, EACH TIME I STARTED TO SAY IT

All evening, each time I started to say it,
something would interrupt.
It was not a thought so very large—
it could in fact have slipped through any window
cracked open a bit for air.
Yet each time I started to say it, at that table,
someone else would speak, the moment would pass.
After the fifth time this happened, I began to be amused.
Runt-of-the-litter thought, I thought, *unable to get to the tit.*
Then suddenly wanted to lift it up,
to feed it an eyedropper's measure of mare's milk,
some warmed sugar water, a little colostrum of badger.
It suddenly seemed to me the kind of thought,
not large, on which a life might turn.
There are many such: unheard, unspoken.
Their blind eyes open and close,
the almost audible valves of their hearts.
But all evening, each time I started to say it,
something would interrupt, the moment would pass.

LADDER

A man tips back his chair, all evening.

Years later, the ladder of small indentations
still marks the floor. Walking across it, then stopping.

Rarely are what is spoken and what is meant the same.

Mostly the mouth says one thing, the thighs and knees
say another, the floor hears a third.

Yet within us,
objects and longings are not different.
They twist on the stem of the heart, like ripening grapes.

BALANCE

Balance is noticed most when almost failed of—

in an elephant's delicate wavering
on her circus stool, for instance,
or that moment
when a ladder starts to tip but steadies back.

There are, too, its mysterious departures.

Hours after the dishes are washed and stacked,
a metal bowl clangs to the floor,
the weight of drying water all that altered;
a painting vertical for years
one morning—*why?*—requires a restoring tap.

You have felt it disappearing
from your own capricious heart—
a restlessness enters, the smallest leaning begins.

Already then inevitable,
the full collision,
the life you will describe afterwards always as "after."

A CEDARY FRAGRANCE

Even now,
decades after,
I wash my face with cold water—

Not for discipline,
nor memory,
nor the icy, awakening slap,

but to practice
choosing
to make the unwanted wanted.

IDENTITY

Decades after a man leaves the Church,
still he is called the priest.

Many years since she set down her bow,
a woman remains the cellist.

The one who seduced so many is content
now to sip her tea,
and still she is looked at with envy and hatred.

The one who held life and death
in his mouth
no longer speaks at all, yet still he is feared.

The unmoving dancer rehearses her steps.
Again, perfection eludes her.

Fate loosens its grip. The bruises stay.

FOR HORSES, HORSEFLIES

We know nothing of the lives of others.
Under the surface, what strange desires,
what rages, weaknesses, fears.

Sometimes it breaks into the daily paper
and we shake our heads in wonder—
"Who would behave in such a way?" we ask.

Unspoken the thought, "Let me not be tested."
Unspoken the thought, "Let me not be known."

Under the surface, something that whispers,
"Anything can be done."

For horses, horseflies. For humans, shame.

MOMENT

A person wakes from sleep
and does not know for a time
who she is, who he is.

This happens in a lifetime
once or twice.
It has happened to you, no doubt.

Some in that moment
panic,
some sigh with pleasure.

How each later envies the other,
who must so love their lives.

SPEED AND PERFECTION

How quickly the season of apricots is over—
a single night's wind is enough.
I kneel on the ground, lifting one, then the next.
Eating those I can, before the bruises appear.

OPTIMISM

More and more I have come to admire resilience.
Not the simple resistance of a pillow, whose foam
returns over and over to the same shape, but the sinuous
tenacity of a tree: finding the light newly blocked on one side,
it turns in another. A blind intelligence, true.
But out of such persistence arose turtles, rivers,
mitochondria, figs—all this resinous, unretractable earth.

TREE

It is foolish
to let a young redwood
grow next to a house.

Even in this
one lifetime,
you will have to choose.

That great calm being,
this clutter of soup pots and books—

Already the first branch-tips brush at the window.
Softly, calmly, immensity taps at your life.

THE SILENCE

One acquaintance says of another,
"I think he's a happy man,"
then pauses.

I see on his face what I also
am thinking,
and wonder what he is remembering,
inside our silence.

I am remembering a funeral,
friend after friend rising to speak
of the lost one.
I did not know him well,
yet still, by one thing he had told me,
wore fully our closeness.

Or perhaps it was even simpler—
to whom else could he say the truth?

I wondered, even then,
how many others attending knew also one thing.
Each secret separate, different,
leading its life now without him:
carrying laundry, washing the windows, straightening up.

As they do, perhaps, I would like to sit down now and rest.

I would like to ponder the flavor
of how much I know of others, how much I do not;
of what of me is known and what is not.

A conversation is overheard on a train, on an airplane,
and even Love cannot know the whole.
It sits in the row behind,

listening quietly to what it is able.
Then the green and red wing-lights blink out;
the train rounds the track's curve and is lost.

Love, also disappearing,
would like to tap the two murmuring ones on the shoulder.
Love would like to say to them,
"Speak more fearlessly—this is the only—say what you can."

Politeness forbids it.

Love sits in the row behind,
and quietly listens.
Love lowers its stricken face so no one will see.

SLEEP

Horses, yes.
Dogs, old ones especially.
People of course.
Even trees.

Planets, atoms, do not.
Bacterium, virus?
Unlikely.

Pens sleep
most of the time,
but awaken quickly—
one shake
or a few dry strokes suffice.

A fire sleeps by dark,
a cat by daylight,
each curled in a warming circle.
A rock lies still or tumbles,
but cannot sleep.

Does the wool
sleep along with its sheep?
The hoof with its cow?

The finger sleeps
and the ring does not—
what of the vow?

A woman touched by a man
pretends, sometimes,
to sleep,
for the pleasure of letting him think
that she awakens.

After, her thighs
sleep differently than before.

Sometimes the heart
goes sleepless or sleeps for years;
sometimes the mind.

I have tried to talk
with my sleep,
to ask it politely for this or that,
but it only averts its gaze.

"Go away," it says,
and, "Leave me alone."
As if without me
it could be anything at all.

Still, it knows who is slave,
who master.

And so I lavish on it
goosedown and soft cotton,
offer it sweetened milk
or wine,
tuck it into warm blankets
under a window opened just an inch.

Some speak
of entering sleep,
but it is sleep that enters us,
as a farmer, familiar,
confident, enters his field.

Night after night it tills and waters,
so that at times we awaken
buoyant,
other times in inexplicable grief.

And though the child
who refuses to sleep
is right perhaps to be inconsolable—
begging more time,
clutching her bear to her cheek—
she too will finally agree.

Joining the silent magpies
and tough-skinned conch and saguaro;
the swaying mule deer,
suspended pipefish,
and deep-sighing maple—

all who, drifting,
distal,
quilt the drowsy night-song of the mortal.

INK

Like all liquids,
it is sister to chaos and time:
wanting always
to lose itself in another,
visible only when held in embrace.

It is also like the aurochs
of ancient Europe,
reentering the world with reluctance—
at the threshold, marks of the scoring horns,
their curls, tip-blots, and scratchings.

Some of its substances:

Carbon of lampblack.
Lapis well-powdered.
Rust flakes milled fine.

Certain inks grip their surface,
others soak in.
Still others, like potters' glazes,
require baking—
the paper arrives warm then with its words,
a fresh bread seeded with poppies.

The tulip magnolia
writes first in white ink, then in green.
Each new twig blossoms as ink to the reading mind.

As with the squid's dark cloud
or the writings on certain moth-wings,
some inks are meant to disguise—
the eye of the hawk stares fiercely,
but where is the hawk?

Some glossy, brilliant, expounding,
others darkly impenetrable as sleep,
all consist of pigment, binder, and carrier.

Each part must be compatible with the others.
And so the glueing binder—
shellac, gum arabic, plastic, or resin—
must enter seamlessly
into the carrier's solvent.
In this, ink is like a metaphor well-made.

And like metaphor,
good ink has also its fragrance:
some smell of earth,
others are heady with spirits.

In itself ink is carrier, solvent,
and pigment to thought:
thought, entering ink,
equally transports, rushes, and stays.

Alcohol-based, oil-based, or water,
all inks must eventually dry,
releasing their words from the verb-tense
of present-resilient to that of perfected past.

They settle weightless, meaningful as dust.

Until the reader—
an aromatic organic carrier
not unlike any other,
not unlike, say, fresh turpentine meeting old varnish—
re-dissolves them,
adds back the moistened eye, the moistened mind.

Then the drying and non-drying oils—
petroleum, soya—
unfasten their chemical binding.
The script-melisma unscrolls in the listening ear.

And again the impossible
happens with such ease it is almost unnoticed:

A radish once dipped
in salt and eaten is eaten once more.
A mountain walks in and out of its quantum of fog.
A woman of ancient China paints dark her eyebrows.

Then each grain of that salt
passes again through the world-gate,
returned to the black gates of ink, which silently close.

METEMPSYCHOSIS

Some stories last many centuries,
others only a moment.
All alter over that lifetime like beach-glass,
grow distant and more beautiful with salt.

Yet even today, to look at a tree
and ask the story *Who are you?* is to be transformed.

There is a stage in us where each being, each thing, is a mirror.

Then the bees of self pour from the hive-door,
ravenous to enter the sweetness of flowering nettles and thistle.

Next comes the ringing a stone or violin or empty bucket
gives off—
the immeasurable's continuous singing,
before it goes back into story and feeling.

In Borneo, there are palm trees that walk on their high roots.
Slowly, with effort, they lift one leg then another.

I would like to join that stilted transmigration,
to feel my own skin vertical as theirs:
an ant road, a highway for beetles.

I would like not minding, whatever travels my heart.
To follow it all the way into leaf-form, bark-furl, root-touch,
and then keep walking, unimaginably further.

FROM

After

(2006)

AFTER LONG SILENCE

Politeness fades,

a small anchovy gleam
leaving the upturned pot in the dishrack
after the moon has wandered out of the window.

One of the late freedoms, there in the dark.
The left-over soup put away as well.

Distinctions matter. Whether a goat's
quiet face should be called noble
or indifferent. The difference between a right rigor and pride.

The untranslatable thought must be the most precise.

Yet words are not the end of thought, they are where it begins.

THEOLOGY

If the flies did not hurry themselves to the window
they'd still die somewhere.

Other creatures choose the other dimension:
                                        to slip
into a thicket, swim into the shaded, undercut
part of the stream.
                        My dog would make her tennis ball
disappear into just such a hollow,
pushing it under the water with both paws.
Then dig for it furiously, wildly, until it popped up again.

A game or a theology, I could not tell.

The flies might well prefer the dawn-ribboned mouth of a trout,
its crisp and speed,
                        if they could get there,
though they are not in truth that kind of fly
and preference is not given often in these matters.

A border collie's preference is to do anything entirely,
with the whole attention. This Simone Weil called prayer.
And almost always, her prayers were successful—
                                        the tennis ball
could be summoned again to the surface.

When a friend's new pound dog, diagnosed distempered,
doctored for weeks, crawled under the porch to die, my friend crawled after,
pulled her out, said "No!",

as if to live were just a simple matter of training.
                        The coy-dog, startled, obeyed.
Now trots out to greet my car when I come to visit.

Only a firefly's evening blinking outside the window,
this miraculous story, but everyone hurries to believe it.

PYRACANTHA AND PLUM

Last autumn's chastened berries still on one tree,
spring blossoms tender, hopeful, on another.
The view from this window
much as it was ten years ago, fifteen.
Yet it seems this morning
a self-portrait both clearer and darker,
as if while I slept some Rembrandt or Brueghel
had walked through the garden, looking hard.

DOG AND BEAR

The air this morning,
blowing between fog and drizzle,

is like a white dog in the snow
who scents a white bear in the snow
who is not there.

Deeper than seeing,
deeper than hearing,
they stand and glare at one another.

So many listen lost, in every weather.

The mind has mountains,
Hopkins wrote, against his sadness.

The dog held the bear at bay, that day.

THE WOODPECKER KEEPS RETURNING

The woodpecker keeps returning
to drill the house wall.
Put a pie plate over one place, he chooses another.

There is nothing good to eat there:
he has found in the house
a resonant billboard to post his intentions,
his voluble strength as provider.

But where is the female he drums for? Where?

I ask this, who am myself the ruined siding,
the handsome red-capped bird, the missing mate.

VILNIUS

For a long time
I keep the guidebooks out on the table.
In the morning, drinking coffee, I see the spines:
St Petersburg, Vilnius, Vienna.
Choices pondered but not finally taken.
Behind them—sometimes behind thick fog—the mountain.
If you lived higher up on the mountain,
I find myself thinking, what you would see is
more of everything else, but not the mountain.

TO JUDGMENT: AN ASSAY

You change a life
as eating an artichoke changes the taste
of whatever is eaten after.
Yet you are not an artichoke, not a piano or cat—
not objectively present at all—
and what of you a cat possesses is essential but narrow:
to know if the distance between two things can be leapt.
The piano, that good servant,
has none of you in her at all, she lends herself
to what asks; this has been my ambition as well.
Yet a person who has you is like an iron spigot
whose water comes from far-off mountain springs.
Inexhaustible, your confident pronouncements flow,
coldly delicious.
For if judgment hurts the teeth, it doesn't mind,
not judgment. Teeth pass. Pain passes.
Judgment decrees what remains—
the serene judgments of evolution or the judgment
of a boy-king entering Persia: "Burn it," he says,
and it burns. And if a small tear swells the corner
of one eye, it is only the smoke, it is no more to him than a beetle
fleeing the flames of the village with her six-legged children.
The biologist Haldane—in one of his tenderer moments—
judged beetles especially loved by God,
"because He had made so many." For judgment can be tender:
I have seen you carry a fate to its end as softly as a retriever
carries the quail. Yet however much
I admire you at such moments, I cannot love you:
you are too much in me, weighing without pity your own worth.
When I have erased you from me entirely,
disrobed of your measuring adjectives,
stripped from my shoulders and hips each of your nouns,
when the world is horsefly, coal barge, and dawn the color of winter
      butter—
not *beautiful*, not *cold*, only the color of butter—

then perhaps I will love you. Helpless to not.

As a newborn wolf is helpless: no choice but hunt the wolf milk, find it sweet.

TO OPINION: AN ASSAY

Many capacities have been thought to define the human—
yet finches and wasps use tools; speech comes
into this world in many forms.
Perhaps it is you, Opinion.

Though I cannot know for certain,
I doubt the singing dolphins have opinions.

This thought of course, is you.

A mosquito's estimation of her meal, however subtle,
is not an opinion. That's my opinion, too.

To think about you is to step into

> *your arms? a thicket? pitfall?*

When you come rising strongly in me, I feel myself grow separate
and more lonely.
Even when others share you, this is so.

Darwin said no fact or description that fails to support an argument can serve.

Myōe wrote: *Bright, bright, bright, bright, the moon.*

Last night there were whole minutes when you released me.
Ocean ocean ocean was the sound the sand made of the moonlit waves
breaking on it.

I felt no argument with any part of my life.

Not even with you, Opinion, who drifted in salt waters with the bullwhip kelp
and phosphorescent plankton,
nibbling my legs and ribcage to remind me where Others end and I begin.

Good joke, I agreed with you, companion Opinion.

RYOANJI: AN ASSAY

Wherever a person stands in the garden of Ryoanji, there is always a stone that cannot be seen. It is like the sliver of absence found on the face of a man who has glimpsed in himself a thing until then unknown. Inside the silence, just before he begins to weep. Not because of the thing he has learned—monstrous or saintly, it was always within him—but for the amplitude he hadn't believed was there.

"OF": AN ASSAY

Its chain link can be delicate or massive. In the human realm, directional: though one thing also connects to another through "and," this is not the same. Consider: "Science and elephants." "The science of elephants." "The elephants of science." In nature, however, the preposition is bidirectional and equal. The tree that possesses the roots is not different from the root-possessed tree. The flashing red of the hummingbird's crest is the bird; the crust of a bread loaf, the loaf. The interior nonexistent without the external, each part coequal. And so grief too becomes meaningless in that fortunate world.

TO SPEECH: AN ASSAY

This first, this last:
there's nothing you wouldn't say.

Unshockable inclusion your most pure nature,
and so you are like an iron pot—
whatever's put in, it holds.

We think it's the fire that cooks the stew,
but, speech, it's also you:
teacher
of fire-making and stew-making,
orator of all our plans and intentions.

We think we think with a self.
That also, it seems, is mostly you—
sometimes a single spider's thread of you,
sometimes a mountain.

The late sun paints orange
the white belly of a hawk overhead—
that wasn't you,
though now and here, it is.

If a hungry child says "orange," her taste buds grow larger.

If a person undamaged says "hungry child,"
his despondence grows larger.

You are not, of course, omnipotent.
In fact, you do little unaided by muscle, by matter.
And still, present and absent, speech, you change us.

As Issa changed, writing after the death of his daughter,

> *This world of dew*
> *is a world of dew.*
> *And yet.*

How much of you
was left uninvited into those lines.
That silence your shadow, bringing his grieving to me.

For days
I made phone calls to strangers,
the few words repeated over and over,
between the "please, if you have a moment" and "thank you."

I didn't expect to make a difference, and didn't. And yet.

Your vehicles are air and memory,
teeth, tongue, papyrus, woodblocks, iron,
signing fingers, circuits, transistors, and ink.
A wheel is not your vehicle, nor an engine.

Terence was your vehicle,
saying in Latin:
"Whatever is human cannot be foreign to me."

Your own truth as well.
For of all our parts, you are our closest mirror,
growing thin or fat, muscular, clumsy,
speeding or slowing as we do.

The wolf-child without you called wolf-child, not-fully-human.

You are held, in the forms we can know you,
only by creatures
able to pass you to others
living often in sadness and tiredness, sometimes in hope.

A friend, who is sometimes sad, said this:
"To be able to hope means also that we can regret."

You rest, fierce speech, in both.
As well as in bargaining, persuasion, argument, gossip,
flirtation, jokes.

Fear, hunger, rage stammer beyond you:
what lives in words is what words were needed to learn.

And so it is good we sometimes set you down
and walk—
unthinking and peaceful, planning nothing—
by the cold, salt, unobedient, unlistening sea.

Only then, without you, are we able to see you completely,
like those wandering monks
who, calling nowhere home, are everywhere home.

POSSIBILITY: AN ASSAY

Again I looked out the window.
All around me, the morning still dark.

The mountain's outline there, but not the mountain.

Then a neighbor's facing plate-glass filled
with the colors, acute and tender, of a Flemish painting.
Corals, blues.

Which seemed to be a preview of the future but were,
I knew,
this moment simply looking elsewhere,
like a woman who has wept for weeks who realizes
that she is also hungry.

AGAINST CERTAINTY

There is something out in the dark that wants to correct us.
Each time I think "this," it answers "that."
Answers hard, in the heart-grammar's strictness.

If I then say "that," it too is taken away.

Between certainty and the real, an ancient enmity.
When the cat waits in the path-hedge,
no cell of her body is not waiting.
This is how she is able so completely to disappear.

I would like to enter the silence portion as she does.

To live amid the great vanishing as a cat must live,
one shadow fully at ease inside another.

THOSE WHO CANNOT ACT

"Those who act will suffer,
suffer into truth"—
What Aeschylus omitted:
those who cannot act will suffer too.

The sister banished into exile.
The unnamed dog
soon killed.

Even the bystanders vanish,
one by one,
peripheral, in pain unnoticed while

THE DOUBLE

More and more I have come to wonder
about this stranger—
woman whose sweaters and coats resemble my own,

whose taste in breads and coffee
resembles my own,
who sleeps when I sleep, wakens when I awaken.

For her,
whose verb-form takes the felicitous "s" at its close,
what happens is simply what happens.

I fret the most slender of errors—
the name forgotten, the borrowed book unreturned—

but never have found her holding a teacup
or coin between her fingers
as if its substance and purpose were something she did not comprehend.

How self-assured she seems,
who decides nothing,
whose insomnia is to my own what the shadow of a leaf is to a leaf.

I am tired, but she is not tired.
I am wordless;
she, who has never spoken a word of her own,
is full of thoughts as precise and impassioned
as the yellow and black exchanges of a wasp's striped body.

For a long time I thought her imposter.
Then realized:
her jokes, even her puns, are only too subtle for me to follow.

And so we go on, mostly ignoring each other,
though what I cook, she eats with seeming gusto,
and letters intended for her alone I open with a curious ease,
as if I, not she, were the long-accomplished thief.

I IMAGINE MYSELF IN TIME

I imagine myself in time looking back on myself—
this self, this morning,
drinking her coffee on the first day of a new year
and once again almost unable to move her pen through the iron air.
Perplexed by my life as Midas was in his world of sudden metal,
surprised that it was not as he'd expected, what he had asked.
And that other self, who watches me from the distance of decades,
what will she say? Will she look at me with hatred or with compassion,
I whose choices made her what she will be?

LATE SELF-PORTRAIT BY REMBRANDT

The dog, dead for years, keeps coming back in the dream.
We look at each other there with the old joy.
It was always her gift to bring me into the present—

Which sleeps, changes, awakens, dresses, leaves.

Happiness and unhappiness
differ as a bucket hammered from gold differs from one of pressed tin,
this painting proposes.

Each carries the same water, it says.

THE HEAT OF AUTUMN

The heat of autumn
is different from the heat of summer.
One ripens apples, the other turns them to cider.
One is a dock you walk out on,
the other the spine of a thin swimming horse
and the river each day a full measure colder.
A man with cancer leaves his wife for his lover.
Before he goes she straightens his belts in the closet,
rearranges the socks and sweaters inside the dresser
by color. That's autumn heat:
her hand placing silver buckles with silver,
gold buckles with gold, setting each
on the hook it belongs on in a closet soon to be empty,
and calling it pleasure.

BURLAP SACK

A person is full of sorrow
the way a burlap sack is full of stones or sand.
We say, "Hand me the sack,"
but we get the weight.
Heavier if left out in the rain.
To think that the stones or sand are the self is an error.
To think that grief is the self is an error.
Self carries grief as a pack mule carries the side bags,
being careful between the trees to leave extra room.
The mule is not the load of ropes and nails and axes.
The self is not the miner nor builder nor driver.
What would it be to take the bride
and leave behind the heavy dowry?
To let the thin-ribbed mule browse in tall grasses,
its long ears waggling like the tails of two happy dogs?

THE MONK STOOD BESIDE A WHEELBARROW

The monk stood beside a wheelbarrow, weeping.

God or Buddha nowhere to be seen—
these tears were fully human,
bitter, broken,
falling onto the wheelbarrow's rusty side.

They gathered at its bottom,
where the metal drank them in to make more rust.

You cannot know what you do in this life, what you have done.
The monk stood weeping.

I knew I also had a place on this hard earth.

[TEN PEBBLES]

Global Warming

When his ship first came to Australia,
Cook wrote, the natives
continued fishing, without looking up.
Unable, it seemed, to fear what was too large to be comprehended.

The Complaint

"I do not like his most recent book,"
one master said of another.
"It compels weeping."

Maple

The lake scarlets
the same instant as the maple.
Let others try to say this is not passion.

Lemon

The grated lemon rind bitters the oil it steeps in.
A wanted flavor.
Like the moment in love when one lover knows
the other could do anything now wanted, yet does not.

Tool Use in Animals

For a long time it was thought
the birds were warning: Panther! Panther!
Then someone understood. The birds were scavengers.
The cry was, "Human! Human!"

To Sneezing

Pure master of all our losses,
dissolver of self and its zeals—
we bow before you as newspaper bows to the match.

Why Bodhidharma Went to Motel 6

"Where is your home?" the interviewer asked him.

"Here."

"No, no," the interviewer said, thinking it a problem of translation,
"when you are where you actually live?"

Now it was his turn to think, *Perhaps the translation?*

A Class Almost Empty

How did Roget decide
that the opposite of "time" is not
"instantaneity" but "neverness"—
a concept so difficult he could
scarcely think of additional entries,
resorting instead to phrases from Latin and Greek,
too early for the possibility "Birkenau-Auschwitz."

Sentence

The body of a starving horse cannot forget the size it was born to.

Red Scarf

The red scarf
still hangs over the chairback.
In its folds,
like a perfume
that cannot be quite remembered,
inconceivable *before*.

for L.B. 1950–2004

IN A ROOM WITH FIVE PEOPLE, SIX GRIEFS

In a room with five people, six griefs.

Some you will hear of, some not.

Let the room hold them, their fears, their anger.

Let there be walls and windows, a ceiling.

A door through which time

changer of everything

can enter.

"IT IS NIGHT. IT IS VERY DARK."

Rainfall past any interrogation.
Questions and answers are not the business of rain.

Yet I step forward by them—
Left foot? Yes. Right foot? Yes.
And all the time wanting to be soaked through
as the flowers of the apricot that open too early,
in mid-December,
are soaked all the way through their slow petals but do not fall.

The colors only slightly deepen.
The fruit has far to travel.
Left foot by right foot under the hidden stars.

And I?
Question by question,
like an elephant trained to paint what is in her heart.

THE PROMISE

Mysteriously they entered, those few minutes.
Mysteriously, they left.
As if the great dog of confusion guarding my heart,
who is always sleepless, suddenly slept.
It was not any awakening of the large, not so much as that,
only a stepping back from the petty.
I gazed at the range of blue mountains,
I drank from the stream. Tossed in a small stone from the bank.
Whatever direction the fates of my life might travel, I trusted.
Even the greedy direction, even the grieving, trusted.
There was nothing left to be saved from, bliss nor danger.
The dog's tail wagged a little in his dream.

THE BELL ZYGMUNT

For fertility, a new bride is lifted to touch it with her left hand,
or possibly kiss it.
The sound close in, my friend told me later, is almost silent.

At ten kilometers, even those who have never heard it know what it is.

If you stand near during thunder, she said,
you will hear a reply.

Six weeks and six days from the phone's small ringing,
replying was over.

She who cooked lamb and loved wine and wild mushroom pastas.
She who when I saw her last was silent as the great Zygmunt mostly is,
a ventilator's clapper between her dry lips.

Because I could, I spoke. She laid her palm on my cheek to answer.
And soon again, to say it was time to leave.

I put my lips near the place a tube went into
the back of one hand.
The kiss—as if it knew what I did not yet—both full and formal.

As one would kiss the ring of a cardinal, or the rim
of that cold iron bell, whose speech can mean "Great joy,"
or equally, "The city is burning. Come."

THE DEAD DO NOT WANT US DEAD

The dead do not want us dead;
such petty errors are left for the living.
Nor do they want our mourning.
No gift to them—not rage, not weeping.
Return one of them, any one of them, to the earth,
and look: such foolish skipping,
such telling of bad jokes, such feasting!
Even a cucumber, even a single anise seed: feasting.

September 15, 2001

IT WAS LIKE THIS: YOU WERE HAPPY

It was like this:
you were happy, then you were sad,
then happy again, then not.

It went on.
You were innocent or you were guilty.
Actions were taken, or not.

At times you spoke, at other times you were silent.
Mostly, it seems you were silent—what could you say?

Now it is almost over.

Like a lover, your life bends down and kisses your life.

It does this not in forgiveness—
between you, there is nothing to forgive—
but with the simple nod of a baker at the moment
he sees the bread is finished with transformation.

Eating, too, is a thing now only for others.

It doesn't matter what they will make of you
or your days: they will be wrong,
they will miss the wrong woman, miss the wrong man,
all the stories they tell will be tales of their own invention.

Your story was this: you were happy, then you were sad,
you slept, you awakened.
Sometimes you ate roasted chestnuts, sometimes persimmons.

FROM

Come, Thief

(2011)

FRENCH HORN

For a few days only,
the plum tree outside the window
shoulders perfection.
No matter the plums will be small,
eaten only by squirrels and jays.
I feast on the one thing, they on another,
the shoaling bees on a third.
What in this unpleated world isn't someone's seduction?
The boy playing his intricate horn in Mahler's Fifth,
in the gaps between playing,
turns it and turns it, dismantles a section,
shakes from it the condensation
of human passage. He is perhaps twenty.
Later he takes his four bows, his face deepening red,
while a girl holds a viola's spruce wood and maple
in one half-opened hand and looks at him hard.
Let others clap.
These two, their ears still ringing, hear nothing.
Not the shouts of *bravo*, *bravo*,
not the timpanic clamor inside their bodies.
As the plum's blossoms do not hear the bee
nor taste themselves turned into storable honey
by that sumptuous disturbance.

FIRST LIGHT EDGING CIRRUS

10^{25} molecules
are enough
to call woodthrush or apple.

A hummingbird, fewer.
A wristwatch: 10^{24}.

An alphabet's molecules,
tasting of honey, iron, and salt,
cannot be counted—

as some strings, untouched,
sound when a near one is speaking.

So it was when love slipped inside us.
It looked out face to face in every direction.

Then it was inside the tree, the rock, the cloud.

THE DECISION

There is a moment before a shape
hardens, a color sets.
Before the fixative or heat of kiln.
The letter might still be taken
from the mailbox.
The hand held back by the elbow,
the word kept between the larynx pulse
and the amplifying drum-skin of the room's air.
The thorax of an ant is not as narrow.
The green coat on old copper weighs more.
Yet something slips through it—
looks around,
sets out in the new direction, for other lands.
Not into exile, not into hope. Simply changed.
As a sandy track-rut changes when called a Silk Road:
it cannot be after turned back from.

VINEGAR AND OIL

Wrong solitude vinegars the soul,
right solitude oils it.

How fragile we are, between the few good moments.

Coming and going unfinished,
puzzled by fate,

like the half-carved relief
of a fallen donkey, above a church door in Finland.

NARROWNESS

Day after day,
my neighbors' cats in the garden.

Each in a distant spot,
like wary planets.

One brindled gray,
one black and white,
one orange.

They remind of the feelings:
how one cannot know another completely.

The way two cats cannot sleep
in one patch of mint-scented shade.

SHEEP

It is the work of feeling
to undo expectation.

A black-faced sheep
looks back at you as you pass
and your heart is startled
as if by the shadow
of someone once loved.

Neither comforted by this
nor made lonely.

Only remembering
that a self in exile is still a self,
as a bell unstruck for years
is still a bell.

PERISHABLE, IT SAID

Perishable, it said on the plastic container,
and below, in different ink,
the date to be used by, the last teaspoon consumed.

I found myself looking:
now at the back of each hand,
now inside the knees,
now turning over each foot to look at the sole.

Then at the leaves of the young tomato plants,
then at the arguing jays.

Under the wooden table and lifted stones, looking.
Coffee cups, olives, cheeses,
hunger, sorrow, fears—
these too would certainly vanish, without knowing when.

How suddenly then
the strange happiness took me,
like a man with strong hands and strong mouth,
inside that hour with its perishing perfumes and clashings.

LOVE IN AUGUST

White moths
against the screen
in August darkness.

Some clamor
in envy.

Some spread large
as two hands
of a thief

who wants to put
back in your cupboard
the long-taken silver.

BRUISES

In age, the world grows clumsy.

A heavy jar
leaps from a cupboard.
A suitcase has corners.

Others have no explanation.

Old love, old body,
do you remember—
carpet burns down the spine,
gravel bedding
the knees, hardness to hardness.

You who knew yourself
kissed by the bite of the ant,
you who were kissed by the bite of the spider.

Now kissed by this.

THE PROMISE

Stay, I said
to the cut flowers.
They bowed
their heads lower.

Stay, I said to the spider,
who fled.

Stay, leaf.
It reddened,
embarrassed for me and itself.

Stay, I said to my body.
It sat as a dog does,
obedient for a moment,
soon starting to tremble.

Stay, to the earth
of riverine valley meadows,
of fossiled escarpments,
of limestone and sandstone.
It looked back
with a changing expression, in silence.

Stay, I said to my loves.
Each answered,
Always.

CHINA

Whales follow
the whale-roads.
Geese,
roads of magnetized air.

To go great distance,
exactitudes matter.

Yet how often
the heart
that set out for Peru
arrives in China.

Steering hard.
Consulting the charts
the whole journey.

Under each station of the real,
another glimmers.
And so the love of false-bottomed drawers
and the salt mines outside Kraków
going down and down without drowning.
A man harms his wife, his child.
He says, "Here is the reason."
She says, "Here is the reason."
The child says nothing,
watching him led away.
If truth is the lure, humans are fishes.
All the fine bones of that eaten-up story,
think about them.
Their salt-cod whiteness on whiteness.

Seawater stiffens cloth long after it's dried.
As pain after it's ended stays in the body:
A woman moves her hands oddly
because her grandfather passed through
a place he never spoke of. Making
instead the old jokes with angled fingers.
Call one thing another's name long enough,
it will answer. Call pain seawater, tree, it will answer.
Call it a tree whose shape of branches happened.
Call what branching happened a man
whose job it was to break fingers or lose his own.
Call fingers angled like branches what peel and cut apples,
to give to a girl who eats them in silence, looking.
Call her afterward tree, call her seawater angled by silence.

WASHING DOORKNOBS

The glass doorknobs turn no differently.
But every December
I polish them with vinegar water and cotton.

Another year ends.
This one, I ate Kyoto pickles
and touched, in Xi'an, a stone turtle's face,
cold as stone, as turtle.

I could not read the fortune carved into its shell
or hear what it had raised its head
to listen for, such a long time.

Around it, the madness of empires continued,
an unbitted horse that runs for a thousand miles
between grazing.

Around us, the madness of empires continues.

How happy we are,
how unhappy we are, doesn't matter.
The stone turtle listens. The famished horse runs.

Washing doorknobs, one year enters another.

HEAT AND DESPERATION

Preparation, she thought,
as if a pianist,
limbering, stretching.
But fingers are tendon, not spirit;
are bone and muscle and skin.
Increase of reach extends reach,
but not what comes then to fill it.
What comes to fill it is something that has no name,
a hunger from outside the wolf-colored edges.
Thirteen smoke jumpers died at Mann Gulch.
Two ran faster.
One stopped, set a match ahead of himself,
ahead of the fire. Then stepped upslope,
lay down inside still-burning ashes, and lived.

ALZHEIMER'S

When a fine, old carpet
is eaten by mice,
the colors and patterns
of what's left behind
do not change.
As bedrock, tilted,
stays bedrock,
its purple and red striations unbroken.
Unstrippable birthright grandeur.
"How are you," I asked,
not knowing what to expect.
"Contrary to Keatsian joy," he replied.

in memoriam Leonard Nathan

GREEN-STRIPED MELONS

They lie
under stars in a field.
They lie under rain in a field.
Under sun.

Some people
are like this as well—
like a painting
hidden beneath another painting.

An unexpected weight
the sign of their ripeness.

ALL THE DIFFICULT HOURS AND MINUTES

All the difficult hours and minutes
are like salted plums in a jar.
Wrinkled, turned steeply into themselves,
they mutter something the color of sharkfins to the glass.
Just so, calamity turns toward calmness.
First a jar holds the *umeboshi*, then the rice does.

THE PRESENT

I wanted to give you something—
no stone, clay, bracelet,
no edible leaf could pass through.
Even a molecule's fragrance by then too large.
Giving had been taken, as you soon would be.
Still, I offered the puffs of air shaped to meaning.
They remained air.
I offered memory on memory,
but what is memory that dies with the fallible inks?
I offered apology, sorrow, longing. I offered anger.
How fine is the mesh of death. You can almost see through it.
I stood on one side of the present, you stood on the other.

Like Moonlight Seen in a Well

Like moonlight seen in a well.

The one who sees it
blocks it.

Mountain and Mouse

Both move.
One only more slowly.

Memorial

When hearing went, you spoke more.
A kindness.

Now I must.

Everything Has Two Endings

Everything has two endings—
a horse, a piece of string, a phone call.

Before a life, air.
And after.

As silence is not silence, but a limit of hearing.

The Cloudy Vase

Past time,
I threw the flowers out,
washed out
the cloudy vase.

How easily
the old clearness
leapt,
like a practiced tiger,
back inside it.

The Lost Love Poems of Sappho

The poems we haven't read must be her fiercest:
imperfect, extreme. As it is with love,
its nights, its days.
It stands on the top of the mountain
and looks for more mountain, steeper pitches.
Descent a thought impossible to imagine.

It Must Be Leaves

Too slow for rain,
too large for tears,
and grief
cannot be seen.
It must be leaves.
But broken
ones, and brown,
not green.

The Perfection of Loss

Like a native speaker
returned
after long exile,
quiet now in two tongues.

The Visible Heat

Near even a candle, the visible heat.
So it is with a person in love:
buying bread, paying a bridge toll.
You too have been that woman,
the one who is looked at and the one who looks.
Each lowers the eyes before it, without knowing why.

Rainstorm Visibly Shining in the Left-out Spoon of a Leaf

Like grief
in certain peoples' lives:
as if something
still depended on the straightness of the spine.

Sonoma Fire

Large moon the deep orange of embers.
Also the scent.
The griefs of others—beautiful, at a distance.

Night and Day

Who am I is the question of owls.
Crow says, *Get up.*

Opening the Hands Between Here and Here

On the dark road, only the weight of the rope.
Yet the horse is there.

A BLESSING FOR WEDDING

Today when persimmons ripen
Today when fox-kits come out of their den into snow
Today when the spotted egg releases its wren song
Today when the maple sets down its red leaves
Today when windows keep their promise to open
Today when fire keeps its promise to warm
Today when someone you love has died
    or someone you never met has died
Today when someone you love has been born
    or someone you will not meet has been born
Today when rain leaps to the waiting of roots in their dryness
Today when starlight bends to the roofs of the hungry and tired
Today when someone sits long inside his last sorrow
Today when someone steps into the heat of her first embrace
Today, let day and dark bless you
With binding of seed and rind bless you
With snow-chill and lavender bless you
Let the vow of this day keep itself wildly and wholly
Spoken and silent, surprise you inside your ears
Sleeping and waking, unfold itself inside your eyes
Let its fierceness and tenderness hold you
Let its vastness be undisguised in all your days

The mandarin silence of windows before their view,
like guards who nod to every visitor,
"Pass."

"Come, thief,"
the path to the doorway agrees.

A fire requires its own conflagration.
As birth does. As love does.
Saying to time to the end, "Dear one, enter."

FOR THE *LOBARIA*, *USNEA*, WITCHES' HAIR, MAP LICHEN, BEARD LICHEN, GROUND LICHEN, SHIELD LICHEN

Back then, what did I know?
The names of subway lines, buses.
How long it took to walk twenty blocks.

Uptown and downtown.
Not north, not south, not you.

When I saw you, later, seaweed reefed in the air,
you were gray-green, incomprehensible, old.
What you clung to, hung from: old.
Trees looking half-dead, stones.

Marriage of fungi and algae,
chemists of air,
changers of nitrogen-unusable into nitrogen-usable.

Like those nameless ones
who kept painting, shaping, engraving,
unseen, unread, unremembered.
Not caring if they were no good, if they were past it.

Rock wools, water fans, earth scale, mouse ears, dust,
ash–of–the–woods.
Transformers unvalued, uncounted.
Cell by cell, word by word, making a world they could live in.

Leave a door open long enough,
a cat will enter.
Leave food, it will stay.
Soon, on cold nights,
you'll be saying "excuse me"
if you want to get out of your chair.
But one thing you'll never hear from a cat
is "excuse me."
Nor Einstein's famous theorem.
Nor "The quality of mercy is not strained."
In the dictionary of Cat, mercy is missing.
In this world where much is missing,
a cat fills only a cat-sized hole.
Yet your whole body turns toward it
again and again because it is there.

CONTENTMENT

I had lived on this earth
more than fifty years
before hearing the sound
of sixteen New Hampshire Reds
settling in before sleep.
Dusk gathered
like a handkerchief
into a pouch
of clean straw.
But only fifteen
adjusted themselves
on the wooden couch.
One, with more white in her feathers
than the feathers of others,
still wandered outside,
away from the chuckling,
some quiet joke
neither she nor I quite heard.
"The foxes will have you," I told her.
She scratched the ground,
found a late insect to feast on,
set her clipped beak to peck at my shoe.
Reached for, she ran.
Ran from the ramp
I herded her toward as well.
I tried *raccoons*, then *cold*.
I tried *stew*.
She found a fresh seed.
Her legs were white and clean
and appeared very strong.
We ran around the coop
that way a long time,
she seeming delighted, I flapping.
Darkness, not I, brought her in.

THE EGG HAD FROZEN, AN ACCIDENT.
I THOUGHT OF MY LIFE.

The egg had frozen, an accident.
I thought of my life.
I heated the butter anyhow.
The shell peeled easily,
inside it looked
both translucent and boiled.
I moved it around in the pan.
It melted, the whites
first clearing to liquid,
then turning solid
and white again like good laundry.
The yolk kept its yolk shape.
Not fried, not scrambled,
in the end it was cooked.
With pepper and salt, I ate it.
My life that resembled it ate it.
It tasted like any other wrecked thing,
eggish and tender, a banquet.

THE KIND MAN

I sold my grandfather's watch,
its rosy gold and stippled pattern
to be melted.
Movement unreparable.
Lid missing.
Chain—there must have been one—
missing.
The numbers painted
with a single, expert bristle.
I touched the winding stem
before I passed it over the counter.
The kind man took it,
what I'd brought him as if to the Stasi.
He weighed the honey of time.

A DAY IS VAST

A day is vast.
Until noon.
Then it's over.

Yesterday's pondwater
braided still wet in my hair.

I don't know what time is.

You can't ever find it.
But you can lose it.

STONE AND KNIFE

One angle blunts, another sharpens.
Loss also: stone & knife.

Some griefs augment the heart,
enlarge;
some stunt.

Scentless loosestrife,
rooms unwalked in,
these losses are small.

Others cannot be described at all.

POMPEII

How many houses
become a living Pompeii,
undusted, unemptied.

Catastrophe is not only sudden.
Hearts stop in more ways than one.

Sometimes the house key is lost,
sometimes the lock.
Sometimes an ending means what did not knock.

SUITCASE

One ear is going,
packing its suitcase
early.
It is packing the rain.
It is taking some leaves.
These.

Also that russeting bird
in the cloudying
iris,
blurred as a hand
waving goodbye
is.

MY LUCK

My luck
lay in the road
copper side up
and copper side down
It shone
I passed it by
I turned around
I picked it up
I shook
my beggar's cup
quite full
I left it there
to be refound
I bent down and
I unbent up
copper side down
copper side up
between the air
and ground
left there picked up
My luck

A HAND IS SHAPED FOR WHAT IT HOLDS OR MAKES

A hand is shaped for what it holds or makes.
Time takes what's handed to it then—warm bread, a stone,
a child whose fingers touch the page to keep her place.

Beloved, grown old separately, your face
shows me the changes on my own.
I see the histories it holds, the argument it makes

against the thresh of trees, the racing clouds, the race
of birds and sky birds always lose:
        the lines have ranged, but not the cheek's strong bone.
My fingers touching there recall that place.

Once we were one. Then what time did, and hands, erased
us from the future we had owned.
For some, the future holds what hands release, not make.

We made a bridge. We walked it. Laced
night's sounds with passion.
Owls' pennywhistles, after, took our place.

Wasps leave their nest. Wind takes the papery case.
Our wooden house, less easily undone,
now houses others. A life is shaped by what it holds or makes.
I make these words for what they can't replace.

I RAN OUT NAKED IN THE SUN

I ran out naked
in the sun
and who could blame me
who could blame

the day was warm

I ran out naked
in the rain
and who could blame me
who could blame

the storm

I leaned toward sixty
that day almost done
it thundered
then

I wanted more I
shouted *More*
and who could blame me
who could blame

had been before

could blame me
that I wanted more

THE SUPPLE DEER

The quiet opening
between fence strands
perhaps eighteen inches.

Antlers to hind hooves,
four feet off the ground,
the deer poured through.

No tuft of the coarse white belly hair left behind.

I don't know how a stag turns
into a stream, an arc of water.
I have never felt such accurate envy.

Not of the deer:

To be that porous, to have such largeness pass through me.

The Beauty

(2015)

FADO

A man reaches close
and lifts a quarter
from inside a girl's ear,
from her hands takes a dove
she didn't know was there.
Which amazes more,
you may wonder:
the quarter's serrated murmur
against the thumb
or the dove's knuckled silence?
That he found them,
or that she never had,
or that in Portugal,
this same half-stopped moment,
it's almost dawn,
and a woman in a wheelchair
is singing a fado
that puts every life in the room
on one pan of a scale,
itself on the other,
and the copper bowls balance.

MY SKELETON

My skeleton,
who once ached
with your own growing larger

are now,
each year,
imperceptibly smaller,
lighter,
absorbed by your own
concentration.

When I danced,
you danced.
When you broke,
I.

And so it was lying down,
walking,
climbing the tiring stairs.
Your jaws. My bread.

Someday you,
what is left of you,
will be flensed of this marriage.

Angular wristbone's arthritis,
cracked harp of ribcage,
blunt of heel,
opened bowl of the skull,
twin platters of pelvis—
each of you will leave me behind,
at last serene.

What did I know of your days,
your nights,
I who held you all my life

inside my hands
and thought they were empty?

You who held me all your life
in your hands
as a new mother holds
her own unblanketed child,
not thinking at all.

MY PROTEINS

They have discovered, they say,
the protein of itch—
natriuretic polypeptide b—
and that it travels its own distinct pathway
inside my spine.
As do pain, pleasure, and heat.

A body it seems is a highway,
a cloverleaf crossing
well built, well traversed.
Some of me going north, some going south.

Ninety percent of my cells, they have discovered,
are not my own person,
they are other beings inside me.

As ninety-six percent of my life is not my life.

Yet I, they say, am they—
my bacteria and yeasts,
my father and mother,
grandparents, lovers,
my drivers talking on cell phones,
my subways and bridges,
my thieves, my police
who chase my self night and day.

My proteins, apparently also me,
fold the shirts.

I find in this crowded metropolis
a quiet corner,
where I build of not-me Lego blocks
a bench,
pigeons, a sandwich
of rye bread, mustard, and cheese.

It is me and is not,
the hunger
that makes the sandwich good.

It is not me then is,
the sandwich—
a mystery neither of us
can fold, unfold, or consume.

MY SPECIES

even
a small purple artichoke
boiled
in its own bittered
and darkening
waters
grows tender,
grows tender and sweet

patience, I think,
my species

keep testing the spiny leaves

the spiny heart

MY EYES

An hour is not a house,
a life is not a house,
you do not go through them as if
they were doors to another.

Yet an hour can have shape and proportion,
four walls, a ceiling.
An hour can be dropped like a glass.

Some want quiet as others want bread.
Some want sleep.

My eyes went
to the window, as a cat or dog left alone does.

MY WEATHER

Wakeful, sleepy, hungry, anxious,
restless, stunned, relieved.

Does a tree also?
A mountain?

A cup holds
sugar, flour, three large rabbit-breaths

of air.
I hold these.

MY LIFE WAS THE SIZE OF MY LIFE

My life was the size of my life.
Its rooms were room-sized,
its soul was the size of a soul.
In its background, mitochondria hummed,
above it sun, clouds, snow,
the transit of stars and planets.
It rode elevators, bullet trains,
various airplanes, a donkey.
It wore socks, shirts, its own ears and nose.
It ate, it slept, it opened
and closed its hands, its windows.
Others, I know, had lives larger.
Others, I know, had lives shorter.
The depth of lives, too, is different.
There were times my life and I made jokes together.
There were times we made bread.
Once, I grew moody and distant.
I told my life I would like some time,
I would like to try seeing others.
In a week, my empty suitcase and I returned.
I was hungry, then, and my life,
my life, too, was hungry, we could not keep
our hands off   our clothes on
our tongues from

MANY-ROOFED BUILDING IN MOONLIGHT

I found myself
suddenly voluminous,
three-dimensioned,
a many-roofed building in moonlight.

Thought traversed
me as simply as moths might.
Feelings traversed me as fish.

I heard myself thinking,
It isn't the piano, it isn't the ears.

Then heard, too soon, the ordinary furnace,
the usual footsteps above me.

Washed my face again with hot water,
as I did when I was a child.

THINGS KEEP SORTING THEMSELVES

Does the butterfat know it is butterfat,
milk know it's milk?
No.
Something just goes and something remains.

Like a boarding-house table:
men on one side, women on the other.
Nobody planned it.

Plaid shirts next to one another,
talking in accents from the midwest.

Nobody plans to be a ghost.

Later on, the young people sit in the kitchen.

Soon enough, they'll be the ones
to stumble *Excuse me* and quickly withdraw.
But they don't know that.
No one can ever know that.

A COTTONY FATE

Long ago, someone
told me: avoid *or*.

It troubles the mind
as a held-out piece of meat disturbs a dog.

Now I too am sixty.
There was no other life.

I WANTED ONLY A LITTLE

I wanted, I thought, only a little,
two teaspoons of silence—
one for sugar,
one for stirring the wetness.

No.
I wanted a Cairo of silence,
a Kyoto.
In every hanging garden,
mosses and waters.

The directions of silence:
north, west, south, past, future.

It comes through any window
one inch open,
like rain driven sideways.

Grief shifts,
as a grazing horse does,
one leg to the other.

But a horse sleeping
sleeps with all legs locked.

An extra day—

Like the painting's fifth cow,
who looks out directly,
straight toward you,
from inside her black and white spots.

An extra day—

Accidental, surely:
the made calendar stumbling over the real
as a drunk trips over a threshold
too low to see.

An extra day—

With a second cup of black coffee.
A friendly but businesslike phone call.
A mailed-back package.
Some extra work, but not too much—
just one day's worth, exactly.

An extra day—

Not unlike the space
between a door and its frame
when one room is lit and another is not,
and one changes into the other
as a woman exchanges a scarf.

An extra day—

Extraordinarily like any other.
And still
there is some generosity to it,
like a letter re-readable after its writer has died.

AS A HAMMER SPEAKS TO A NAIL

When all else fails,
fail boldly,
fail with conviction,
as a hammer speaks to a nail,
or a lamp left on in daylight.

Say *one*.
If *two* does not follow,
say *three*, if that fails, say *life*,
say *future*.

Lacking *future*
try *bucket*,
lacking *iron*, try *shadow*.

If *shadow* too fails,
if your voice falls and falls and keeps falling,
meets only air and silence,

say *one*, again,
but say it with greater conviction,

as a nail speaks to a picture,
as a hammer left on in daylight.

I Sat in the Sun

I moved my chair into sun
I sat in the sun
the way hunger is moved when called fasting.

The Woman, the Tiger

The woman, the tiger, the door, the man, the choice.

Riddles are soulless.
In them, it is never raining.

I Know You Think I've Forgotten

but today
in rain

without coat without hat

Still Life

Loyalty of a book
to its place on the shelf
in a still life.

Like that,
the old loves continue.

Quartz Clock

The ideas of a physicist
can be turned into useful objects:
a rocket, a quartz clock,
a microwave oven for cooking.

The ideas of poets turn into only themselves,
as the hands of the clock do,
or the face of a person.
It changes, but only more into the person.

Humbling: An Assay

Have teeth.

Away from Home, I Thought of the Exiled Poets

Away from home,
I read the exiled poets—
Ovid, Brecht.

Then set my books that night
near the foot of the bed.

All night pretended they were the cat.

Not once
did I wake her.

Two Linen Handkerchiefs

How can you have been dead twelve years
and these still

Anywhere You Look

in the corner of a high rain gutter
under the roof tiles
new grasses' delicate seed heads

what war, they say

Nothing on two legs weighs much,
or can.
An elephant, a donkey, even a cookstove—
those legs, a person could stand on.
Two legs pitch you forward.
Two legs tire.
They look for another two legs to be with,
to move one set forward to music
while letting the other move back.
They want to carve into a tree trunk:
2gether 4ever.
Nothing on two legs can bark,
can whinny or chuff.
Tonight, though, everything's different.
Tonight I want wheels.

WORKS & LOVES

1.

Rain fell as a glass
breaks,
something suddenly everywhere at the same time.

2.

To live like a painting
looked into from more than one angle at once—

eye to eye with the doorway
down at the hair
up at your own dusty feet.

3.

"This is your house,"
said my bird heart to my heart of the cricket,
and I entered.

4.

The happy see only happiness,
the living see only life,
the young see only the young.

As lovers believe
they wake always beside one also in love.

5.

However often I turned its pages,
I kept ending up
as the same two sentences of the book:

The being of some is: to be. Of others: to be without.

Then I fell back asleep, in Swedish.

6.

A sheep grazing is unimpressed by the mountain
but not by its flies.

7.

The grief
of what hasn't yet happened—

a door closed from inside

the weight of the grass
dividing
an ant's five-legged silence
walking through it.

8.

What is the towel, what is the water,
changes,
though of we three,
only the towel can be held upside down in the sun.

9.

"I was once."
Said not in self-pity or praise.
This dignity we allow barn owl,
ego, oyster.

A CHAIR IN SNOW

A chair in snow
should be
like any other object whited
& rounded

and yet a chair in snow is always sad

more than a bed
more than a hat or house
a chair is shaped for just one thing

to hold
a soul its quick and few bendable
hours

perhaps a king

not to hold snow
not to hold flowers

LIKE THE SMALL HOLE BY THE PATH-SIDE
SOMETHING LIVES IN

Like the small hole by the path-side something lives in,
in me are lives I do not know the names of,

nor the fates of,
nor the hungers of or what they eat.

They eat of me.
Of small and blemished apples in low fields of me
whose rocky streams and droughts I do not drink.

And in my streets—the narrow ones,
unlabeled on the self-map—
they follow stairs down music ears can't follow,

and in my tongue borrowed by darkness,
in hours uncounted by the self-clock,
they speak in restless syllables of other losses, other loves.

There too have been the hard extinctions,
missing birds once feasted on and feasting.

There too must be ideas
like loud machines with tungsten bits that grind the day.

A few escape. A mercy.

They leave behind
small holes that something unweighed by the self-scale lives in.

IN A KITCHEN WHERE MUSHROOMS WERE WASHED

In a kitchen where mushrooms were washed,
the mushroom scent lingers.

As the sea must keep for a long time the scent of the whale.

As a person who's once loved completely,
a country once conquered,
does not release that stunned knowledge.

They must want to be found, those strange-shaped, rising morels,
clownish puffballs.

Lichens have served as a lamp-wick.
Clean-burning coconuts, olives.
Dried salmon, sheep fat, a carcass of petrel set blazing:
light that is fume and abradement.

Unburnable mushrooms are other.
They darken the air they come into.

Theirs the scent of having been traveled, been taken.

ALL SOULS

In Italy, on the day of the dead,
they ring bells,
from every church and village in every direction.
At the usual times, the regular bells of the hour—
eleven strokes, twelve. Oar strokes
lain over and into the bottomless water and air.
But the others? Tuneless, keyless,
rhythm of wings at the door of the hive
when the entrance is suddenly shuttered
and the bees, returned heavy, see
that the world of flowering and pollen is over.
There can be no instruction
to make this. Undimensioned
the tongues of the bells,
the ropes of the bells, their big iron bodies unholy.
Barred from form, barred from bars,
from relation. The beauty—unspeakable—
was beauty. I drank it and thirsted,
I stopped. I ran. Wanted closer in every direction.
Each bell stroke released without memory
or judgment, unviolent, untender. Uncaring.
And yet: existent. Something trembling.
I—who have not known bombardment—
have never heard so naked a claim
of the dead on the living, to know them.

ZERO PLUS ANYTHING IS A WORLD

Four less one is three.

Three less two is one.

One less three
is what, is who,
remains.

The first cell that learned to divide
learned to subtract.

Recipe:
add salt to hunger.

Recipe:
add time to trees.

Zero plus anything
is a world.

This one
and no other,
unhidden,
by each breath changed.

Recipe:
add death to life.

Recipe:
love without swerve what this will bring.

Sister, father, mother, husband, daughter.

Like a cello
forgiving one note as it goes,
then another.

ENTANGLEMENT

A librarian in Calcutta and an entomologist in Prague
sign their moon-faced illicit emails,
"*ton entanglée.*"

No one can explain it.
The strange charm between border collie and sheep,
leaf and wind, the two distant electrons.

There is, too, the matter of a horse race.
Each person shouts for his own horse louder,
confident in the rising din
past whip, past mud,
the horse will hear his own name in his own quickened ear.

Desire is different:
desire is the moment before the race is run.

Has an electron never refused
the invitation to change direction,
sent in no knowable envelope, with no knowable ring?

A story told often: after the lecture, the widow
insisting the universe rests on the back of a turtle.
And what, the physicist
asks, does the turtle rest on?

Very clever, young man, she replies, very clever,
but it's turtles all the way down.

And so a woman in Beijing buys for her love,
who practices turtle geometry in Boston, a metal trinket
from a night-market street stall.

On the back of a turtle, at rest on its shell,
a turtle.
Inside that green-painted shell, another, still smaller.

This continues for many turtles,
until finally, too small to see
or to lift up by its curious, preacherly head
a single un-green electron
waits the width of a world for some weightless message
sent into the din of existence for it alone.

Murmur of all that is claspable, clabberable, clamberable,
against all that is not:

You are there. I am here. I remember.

LIKE TWO NEGATIVE NUMBERS MULTIPLIED BY RAIN

Lie down, you are horizontal.
Stand up, you are not.

I wanted my fate to be human.

Like a perfume
that does not choose the direction it travels,
that cannot be straight or crooked, kept out or kept.

Yes, No, Or
—a day, a life, slips through them,
taking off the third skin,
taking off the fourth.

The logic of shoes becomes at last simple,
an animal question, scuffing.

Old shoes, old roads—
the questions keep being new ones.
Like two negative numbers multiplied by rain
into oranges and olives.

FROM

Ledger

(2020)

LET THEM NOT SAY

Let them not say: we did not see it.
We saw.

Let them not say: we did not hear it.
We heard.

Let them not say: they did not taste it.
We ate, we trembled.

Let them not say: it was not spoken, not written.
We spoke,
we witnessed with voices and hands.

Let them not say: they did nothing.
We did not-enough.

Let them say, as they must say something:

A kerosene beauty.
It burned.

Let them say we warmed ourselves by it,
read by its light, praised,
and it burned.

THE BOWL

If meat is put into the bowl, meat is eaten.

If rice is put into the bowl, it may be cooked.

If a shoe is put into the bowl,
the leather is chewed and chewed over,
a sentence that cannot be taken in or forgotten.

A day, if a day could feel, must feel like a bowl.
Wars, loves, trucks, betrayals, kindness,
it eats them.

Then the next day comes, spotless and hungry.

The bowl cannot be thrown away.
It cannot be broken.

It is calm, uneclipsable, rindless,
and, big though it seems, fits exactly in two human hands.

Hands with ten fingers,
fifty-four bones,
capacities strange to us almost past measure.
Scented—as the curve of the bowl is—
with cardamom, star anise, long pepper, cinnamon, hyssop.

AS IF HEARING HEAVY FURNITURE
MOVED ON THE FLOOR ABOVE US

As things grow rarer, they enter the ranges of counting.
Remain this many Siberian tigers,
that many African elephants. Three hundred red-legged egrets.
We scrape from the world its tilt and meander of wonder
as if eating the last burned onions and carrots from a cast-iron pan.
Closing eyes to taste better the char of ordinary sweetness.

ANTS' NEST

"On Being the Right Size," Haldane's short essay is titled.

An ants' nest can be found at the top of a redwood.

No bird that weighs less than ___.
No insect more than ___.
The minimum mass for a whale, for a language, an ice cap.

In a human-sized room,
someone is setting a human-sized table with yellow napkins,
someone is calling
her children to come in from a day whose losses as yet remain child-sized.

TODAY, ANOTHER UNIVERSE

The arborist has determined:
senescence   beetles   canker
quickened by drought
                              but in any case
not prunable   not treatable   not to be propped.

And so.

The branch from which the sharp-shinned hawks and their mate-cries.

The trunk where the ant.

The red squirrels' eighty-foot playground.

The bark   cambium   pine-sap   cluster of needles.

The Japanese patterns   the ink-net.

The dapple on certain fish.

Today, for some, a universe will vanish.
First noisily,
then just another silence.

The silence of *after*, once the theater has emptied.

Of bewilderment after the glacier,
the species, the star.

Something else, in the scale of quickening things,
will replace it,

this hole of light in the light, the puzzled birds swerving around it.

CATACLYSM

It begins subtly:
the maple
withdraws an inch from the birch tree.

The porcupine
wants nothing to do with the skink.

Fish unschool,
sheep unflock to separately graze.

Clouds meanwhile
declare to the sky
they have nothing to do with the sky,
which is not visible as they are,

nor knows the trick of turning
into infant, tumbling pterodactyls.

The turtles and moonlight?
Their long arrangement is over.

As for the humans.
Let us not speak of the humans.
Let us speak of their language.

The first-person singular
condemns the second-person plural
for betrayals neither has words left to name.

The fed consider the hungry
and stay silent.

FECIT

for a person in love, the air looks no different

for a person in grief

in this my one lifetime,
while reading, arguing, cherishing, washing, watching a video, sleeping,
the numbers unseeably rise—

305 ppm, 317 ppm, 390, 400

shin of high granite ticks snow-less the compound fracture

I who wrote this

like the old painters
sign this:

JH fecit.

DAY BEGINNING WITH SEEING THE INTERNATIONAL SPACE STATION AND A FULL MOON OVER THE GULF OF MEXICO AND ALL ITS INVISIBLE FISHES

None of this had to happen.
Not Florida. Not the ibis's beak. Not water.
Not the horseshoe crab's empty body and not the living starfish.
Evolution might have turned left at the corner and gone down another
     street entirely.
The asteroid might have missed.
The seams of limestone need not have been susceptible to sand and
     mangroves.
The radio might have found a different music.
The hips of one man and the hips of another might have stood beside
each other on a bus in Aleppo and recognized themselves as long-lost
     brothers.
The key could have broken off in the lock and the nail-can refused its lid.
I might have been the fish the brown pelican swallowed.
You might have been the way the moon kept not setting long after we
     thought it would,
long after the sun was catching inside the low wave curls coming in
at a certain angle. The light might not have been eaten again by its moving.
If the unbearable were not weightless we might yet buckle under the grief
of what hasn't changed yet. Across the world a man pulls a woman from
     the water
from which the leapt-from overfilled boat has entirely vanished.
From the water pulls one child, another. Both are living and both will
     continue to live.
This did not have to happen. No part of this had to happen.

PRACTICE

I touch my toes.

When I was a child,
this was difficult.
Now I touch my toes daily.

In 2012, in Sanford, Florida,
someone nearby was touching her toes before bed.

Three weeks ago,
in the Philippines or Myanmar, someone was stretching.

Tomorrow, someone elsewhere will bend
first to one side, then the other.

I also do ten push-ups, morning and evening.

Women's push-ups,
from the knees.
They resemble certain forms of religious bowing.

In place of *one*, *two*, *four*, *seven*,
I count the names of incomprehension: *Sanford*, *Ferguson*, *Charleston*.
Aleppo, *Sarajevo*, *Nagasaki*.

I never reach: *Troy*, *Ur*.

I have done this for years now.
Bystander, listener. One of the lucky.
I do not seem to grow stronger.

WORDS

Words are loyal.
Whatever they name they take the side of.
As the word *courage* will afterward grip just as well
the frightened girl soldier who stands on one side of barbed wire,
the frightened boy soldier who stands on the other.
Death's clay, they look at each other with wide-open eyes.
And words—that love peace, love gossip—refuse to condemn them.

SHE BREATHES IN THE SCENT

As the front of a box would miss the sides,
the back,

the grief of the living
misses the grief of the dead.

It is
like a woman who goes to the airport
to meet the planes from a country she long ago lived in.

She knows no passenger but stands near as they exit
still holding their passports.

She breathes in the scent of their clothes.

ENGRAVING: WORLD-TREE WITH AN EMPTY BEEHIVE
ON ONE BRANCH

A too-beautiful view rejects the mind.
It is like a person with a garrulous mouth but no ears.

When Bashō finished his months of walking,
he took off his used-up sandals,
let them fall.

One turned into the scent of withered chrysanthemum,
the other walked out of the story.

It's only after you notice an ache
that you know it must always have been there.
As an actor is there, before he steps in from the wing.

Another of Bashō's haiku:
a long-weathered skull, through whose eyes grow tall, blowing grasses.

They look now into a photograph,
a scraped field in France, September 1916:
men bending, smoking, gleaning the harrowed rucksacks for letters.

War, walking, chrysanthemum, sandal, wheat field, bee smoke of camera
     lens, war.

They're in the past, yet we just keep traveling toward them, then away,
carrying with us the remnant, salvageable,

refugee honey.

NOW A DARKNESS IS COMING

I hold my life with two hands.
I walk with two legs.
Two ears are enough to hear Bach with.

Blinded in one eye, a person sees with the other.

Now a great darkness is coming.
A both-eyes darkness.

I have one mouth.
It holds two words.
Yes, No,
inside all others.

Yes. No. No. Yes.

I say yes to these words, as I must,
and I also refuse them.

My two legs,
shaped to go forward,
obedient to can't-know and must-be,
walk into the time that is coming.

MY DOUBT

I wake, doubt, beside you,
like a curtain half-open.

I dress doubting,
like a cup
undecided if it has been dropped.

I eat doubting,
work doubting,
go out to a dubious café with skeptical friends.

I go to sleep doubting myself,
as a herd of goats
sleep in a suddenly gone-quiet truck.

I dream you, doubt,
nightly—
for what is the meaning of dreaming
if not that all we are while inside it
is transient, amorphous, in question?

Left hand and right hand,
doubt, you are in me,
throwing a basketball, guiding my knife and my fork.
Left knee and right knee,
we run for a bus,
for a meeting that surely will end before we arrive.

I would like
to grow content in you, doubt,
as a double-hung window
settles obedient into its hidden pulleys and ropes.

I doubt I can do so:
your own counterweight governs my nights and my days.

As the knob of hung lead holds steady
the open mouth of a window,
you hold me,
my kneeling before you resistant, stubborn,
offering these furious praises
I can't help but doubt you will ever be able to hear.

I WANTED TO BE SURPRISED.

To such a request, the world is obliging.

In just the past week, a rotund porcupine,
who seemed equally startled by me.

The man who swallowed a tiny microphone
to record the sounds of his body,
not considering beforehand how he might remove it.

A cabbage and mustard sandwich on marbled bread.

How easily the large spiders were caught with a clear plastic cup
surprised even them.

I don't know why I was surprised every time love started or ended.
Or why each time a new fossil, Earth-like planet, or war.
Or that no one kept being there when the doorknob had clearly—

What should not have been so surprising:
my error after error, recognized when appearing on the faces of others.

What did not surprise enough:
my daily expectation that anything would continue,
and then that so much did continue, when so much did not.

Small rivulets still flowing downhill when it wasn't raining.
A sister's birthday.

Also, the stubborn, courteous persistence.
That even today *please* means *please*,
good morning is still understood as *good morning*,

and that when I wake up,
the window's distant mountain remains a mountain,
the borrowed city around me is still a city, and standing.

Its alleys and markets, offices of dentists,
drug store, liquor store, Chevron.
Its library that charges—a happy surprise—no fine for overdue books:
Borges, Baldwin, Szymborska, Morrison, Cavafy.

VEST

I put on again the vest of many pockets.

It is easy to forget
which holds the reading glasses,
which the small pen,
which the house keys,
the compass and whistle, the passport.

To forget at last for weeks
even the pocket holding the day
of digging a place for my sister's ashes,
the one holding the day
where someone will soon enough put my own.

To misplace the pocket
of touching the walls at Auschwitz
would seem impossible.
It is not.

To misplace, for a decade,
the pocket of tears.

I rummage and rummage—
transfers
for Munich, for Melbourne,
to Oslo.
A receipt for a Singapore *kopi*.
A device holding music:
Bach, Garcia, Richter, Porter, Pärt.

A woman long dead now
gave me, when I told her I could not sing,
a kazoo.
Now in a pocket.

Somewhere, a pocket
holding a Steinway.
Somewhere, a pocket
holding a packet of salt.

Borgesian vest,
Oxford English Dictionary vest
with a magnifying glass
tucked inside one snapped-closed pocket,
Wikipedia vest, Rosetta vest,
Enigma vest of decoding,
how is it one person can carry
your weight for a lifetime,
one person
slip into your open arms for a lifetime?

Who was given the world,
and hunted for tissues, for chapstick.

BROCADE

All day wondering
if I've become useless.

All day the osprey
white and black,
carrying
big dry sticks without leaves.

Late, I said to my pride,

You think you're the feathered part
of this, do you?

CHANCE DARKENED ME.

Chance darkened me

as a morning darkens,
preparing to rain.

It goes against its arc,
betrays its clock-hands.

The day was a dark-eyed giraffe,
its unfathomable legs
kept walking.

A person is not a day,
not rain,
no gentle eater of high leaves.

I did not keep walking.
The day inside me,
legs and lungs, kept walking.

BRANCH

A clock does not have hands, a face,
tell anything, rightly or wrongly, least of all time.

An empty branch does not long for its nondescript bird.

The bird is not the quick dash
that holds separate the world's *Yes* from the world's *No*.

Is there anywhere on earth one branch that has never been perched on?

That is not what branches exist for. Yet the birds come.

IN ULVIK

He spent his whole life in Ulvik, working as a gardener in
his own orchard.

(of Olav Hauge)

I too would like to work
as a gardener in my own orchard.
Every Friday I would pay myself
a decent, living wage,
taken in foldable cash from my own wallet,
and sometimes, if the weather was bad,
I would give myself the day off
and thank myself for my kindness
and answer myself, It's nothing, nothing, go on now,
put your feet up, find somewhere warm.
And then I would go back into my house
and think of my kindness
and wonder if my gardener was warm now also
and if I was right to let myself
go away from my own orchard's tending
even so briefly, and each of us
might be thinking, too, of the apples,
cold and wet and hanging in outside wind
and fattening on their own trees without us,
and one of us, first, then the other,
might start to wonder a little,
while pushing a cut of cured apple wood into the fire,
about loneliness and separateness and what
it is lives outside one person's skin and inside another's.

ADVICE TO MYSELF

The computer file
of which
I have no recollection
is labeled "advice to myself"

I click it open
look
scroll further down

the screen
stays back-lit and empty

thus I meet myself again
hopeful and useless

a mystery

precisely as I must
have done
on August 19, 2010, 11:08 A.M.

A REAM OF PAPER

I have a ream of paper,
a cartridge of ink,

almonds,
coffee,
a wool scarf for warmth.

Whatever handcuffs the soul,
I have brought here.

Whatever distances the heart,
I have brought here.

A deer rises onto her haunches
to reach for an apple,

though many fallen apples are on the ground.

THE PAW-PAW

A woman speaks to me
of a paw-paw tree.

I have never seen a paw-paw tree.
I have never eaten its fruit.

I nod.
The conversation continues.

So many things
we think we understand,
until we stop to think.

Her life.

My own.

LIKE OTHERS

In the end,
I was like others.
A person.

Sometimes embarrassed,
sometimes afraid.

When "Fire!" was shouted,
some ran toward it,
some away—

I neck-deep among them.

My Longing

My hope, my despair, my longing.

Every pocket I put you in had its hole.
Mouse and moth, too, have their hungers.

I called you my life.

Good dog, I said, good dog, as if we could answer.

My Hunger

The way the high-wire walker
must carry a pole
to make her arms longer

you carried me   I carried you
through this world.

My Contentment

I reject contentment:
into it, inexperienced saints have been seen to vanish,
in a burst of somewhat cloudy light.

Wild Turkeys

Two remnant-dinosaur wild turkeys
walk between silence and silence. Not to themselves a meal of meat.
I, who am to myself also not meat, feed mosquitoes nightly,
though day and night I wait for hunger
to find me its dark wood violin, inside its dark wood case.

Library Book with Many Precisely Turned-down Corners

I unfold carefully the thoughts of one who has come before me,
the way a listening dog's ears
may be seen lifting
to some sound beyond its person's quite understanding.

O Snail

Under the Svalbard ice cap, Carboniferous-era coal seams.
A good farmer rotates her crops.
The crops don't complain. It's the fate of stalks and forests to vanish.
Last year's fires: Australia, Portugal, Greece. This: California.

O snail, wrote Issa, climb Fuji slowly, slowly.

A Strategy

Living by implication:
wherever the ink isn't is moon.

Sixth Extinction

It took with it
the words that could have described it.

Biophilia

Most of us hungry at daybreak, sleepy by dark.
Some slept, one eye open, in water.
Some could trot.
Some of us lived till morning. Some did not.

Obstacle

This body, still walking.
The wind must go around it.

THE LITTLE SOUL POEMS

(after Hadrian)

Amor Fati

Little soul,
you have wandered
lost a long time.

The woods all dark now,
birded and eyed.

Then a light, a cabin, a fire, a door standing open.

The fairy tales warn you:
Do not go in,
you who would eat will be eaten.

You go in. You quicken.

You want to have feet.
You want to have eyes.
You want to have fears.

Kitchen

Little soul,
how useful was hunger.

From whatever it was we fell into,
you and I,
it sprang open our fingers' grip.

Yet a life is not prepared for its ending
like a sliced eggplant,

salted and pressed to let leave from itself what is bitter.

Snow

Little soul,
for you, too,
death is coming.

Was there something
you thought
you needed to do?

Snow
does not walk into a room

and wonder

why.

Harness

Little soul,
you and I will become

the memory
of a memory of a memory.

A horse
released of the traces
forgets the weight of the wagon.

Pelt

Little soul,
the book of your hours
is closing

over its golds,
its reds, your gazing dog,
your rivers, ladders,
ribcage.

A life
turns into its patterns and perfumes,
then into its pelt.

I don't know now
if we were one, if we were two,
a stippling.

Whither thou goest,
we'd said.

   Rust Flakes on Wind

Little soul,
a day comes when retrospection ceases.

A person falling does not, mid-plummet, look up.

Still,
for a few seconds on Wednesday,
"Where are my truck keys?"

On Thursday, on Sunday: "Where are my truck keys?"

   Wood. Salt. Tin.

Little soul,
do you remember?

You once walked
over wooden boards
to a house
that sat on stilts in the sea.

It was early.

The sun painted
brightness onto the water,

and wherever you sat
that path
led directly to you.

Some mornings
the sea-road was muted
scratched tin,
some mornings blinding.

Then it would leave.

Little soul,
it is strange—
even now it is early.

I Said

I said   I believed
a world without you unimaginable.

Now cutting its flowers to go with you into the fire.

Tchaikovsky's *Eugene Onegin* is 3,592 measures.
A voice kept far from feeling is heard as measured.
What's wanted in desperate times are desperate measures.
Pushkin's unfinished *Onegin*: 5,446 lines.

No visible tears measure the pilot's grief
as she Lidars the height of an island: five feet.
Fifty, its highest leaf.
She logs the years, the weathers, the tree has left.

A million fired-clay bones—animal, human—
set down in a field as protest
measure 400 yards long, 60 yards wide, weigh 112 tons.
The length and weight and silence of the bereft.

Bees do not question the sweetness of what sways beneath them.
One measure of distance is meters. Another is *li*.
Ten thousand li can be translated: "far."
For the exiled, *home* can be translated "then," translated "scar."

One liter
of Polish vodka holds twelve pounds of potatoes.
What we care about most, we call *beyond measure*.
What matters most, we say *counts*. Height now is treasure.

On this scale of one to ten, where is eleven?
Ask all you wish, no twenty-fifth hour will be given.
Measuring mounts—like some Western bar's mounted elk head—
our cataloged vanishing unfinished heaven.

On the fifth day
the scientists who studied the rivers
were forbidden to speak
or to study the rivers.

The scientists who studied the air
were told not to speak of the air,
and the ones who worked for the farmers
were silenced,
and the ones who worked for the bees.

Someone, from deep in the Badlands,
began posting facts.

The facts were told not to speak
and were taken away.
The facts, surprised to be taken, were silent.

Now it was only the rivers
that spoke of the rivers,
and only the wind that spoke of its bees,

while the unpausing factual buds of the fruit trees
continued to move toward their fruit.

The silence spoke loudly of silence,
and the rivers kept speaking
of rivers, of boulders and air.

Bound to gravity, earless and tongueless,
the untested rivers kept speaking.

Bus drivers, shelf stockers,
code writers, machinists, accountants,
lab techs, cellists kept speaking.

They spoke, the fifth day,
of silence.

No wind, no rain,
the tree
just fell, as a piece of fruit does.

But no, not fruit. Not ripe.
Not fell.

It broke. It shattered.

One cone's
addition of resinous cell-sap,
one small-bodied bird
arriving to tap for a beetle.

It shattered.

What word, what act,
was it we thought did not matter?

GHAZAL FOR THE END OF TIME

(after Messiaen)

Break anything—a window, a piecrust, a glacier—it will break open.
A voice cannot speak, cannot sing, without lips, teeth, lamina propria
    coming open.

Some breakage can barely be named, hardly be spoken.
Rains stopped, roof said. Fires, forests, cities, cellars peeled open.

Tears stopped, eyes said. An unhearable music fell instead from them.
A clarinet stripped of its breathing, the cello abandoned.

The violin grieving, a hand too long empty held open.
The imperial piano, its 89th, 90th, 91st strings unsummoned, unwoken.

Watching, listening, was like that: the low, wordless humming of being
    unwoven.
Fish vanished. Bees vanished. Bats whitened. Arctic ice opened.

Hands wanted more time, hands thought we had time. Spending time's
    rivers,
its meadows, its mountains, its instruments tuning their silence, its deep
    mantle broken.

Earth stumbled within and outside us.
Orca, thistle, kestrel withheld their instruction.

Rock said, Burning Ones, pry your own blindness open.
Death said, Now I too am orphan.

MOUNTAINAL

This first-light mountain, its east peak and west peak.

Its first-light creeks:
Lagunitas, Redwood, Fern. Their fishes and mosses.

Its night and day hawk-life, slope-life, fogs, coyote, tan oaks,
white-speckled amanita. Its spiderwebs' sequins.

To be personal is easy:
Wake. Slip arms and legs from sleep into name, into story.

I wanted to be mountainal, wateral, wrenal.

MY DEBT

Like all
who believe in the senses,
I was an accountant,
copyist,
statistician.

Not registrar:
witness.

Permitted to touch
the leaf of a thistle,
the trembling
work of a spider.

To ponder the Hubble's recordings.

It did not matter
if I believed in
the party of particle or of wave,
as I carried no weapon.

It did not matter if I believed.

I weighed ashes,
actions,
cities that glittered like rubies,
on the scales I was given,
calibrated
in units of fear and amazement.

I wrote the word *it*, the word *is*.

I entered the debt that is owed to the real.

Forgive,
spine-covered leaf, soft-bodied spider,

octopus lifting
one curious tentacle back toward the hand of the diver,
that in such black ink
I set down your flammable colors.

Acknowledgments

ACKNOWLEDGMENTS

My debts are beyond measure. Profound gratitude to the many journals, editors, and book publishers whose support of my work over fifty year led to this volume's existence, and especially to: Ted and Renée Weiss and The Quarterly Review of Literature Poetry Series; Jeanette Hopkins and Wesleyan University Press; Hugh van Dusen and HarperCollins; Neil Astley and Bloodaxe Books; Deborah Garrison and Knopf. To all the editorial assistants, designers, copy-editors, typesetters, book printers, paper makers, ink makers, warehouse workers, truck drivers, booksellers —my deepest thanks. Gratitude also to the Guggenheim Foundation, National Endowment for the Arts, and Academy of American Poets, for major fellowships allowing new directions of exploration, and to the residencies and retreat programs whose offered periods of intense seclusion have been life-changing and indispensable: Civitella Ranieri, the Corporation of Yaddo, the Djerassi Resident Artists Program, the MacDowell Colony, the Rauschenberg Foundation's Residency on Captiva, and the Rockefeller Foundation's Bellagio Study Center for Scholars and Artists. And to my family, life companions, and friends beyond naming, both here and departed: thank you.

Grateful acknowledgment also to the journals and anthologies in which poems newly published in this book appeared:

JOURNALS: *The Alaska Quarterly Review*: "Thermopolium"; *Alta*: "Poem to Be Written by Magnet in Oil for an Exhibit at the Museum of Tomorrow in Rio de Janeiro"; *The American Poetry Review*: "A Day Just Ends," "Body, Mind of the Ransacked Thrift Shop," "Each Morning Calls Us to Praise This World That Is Fleeting," "Poem Holding a Wristwatch Belonging to the Brazilian Poet Ferreira Gullar"; *The Atlantic*: "Invitation"; *Daedalus*: "O, Responsibility"; *Gwarlingo, The Sunday Poem*: "I Would Like"; *The Nation*: "'A map grows no trees.'"; *The New York Review of Books*: "Two Kerosene Lanterns"; *The New Yorker*: "Manifest," "Tin"; *Orion*: "My Window" (as "The Age of Maples"); *Ploughshares*: "Here & Now," "Door & Sentence"; *Plume*: "I open the window."; *Poetry London* (UK): "Body, Mind of the Ransacked Thrift Shop"; *The Red Letters*: "Letter to Adam Zagajewski"; *The San Francisco Chronicle*: "Today, When I Could Do Nothing"; *Scientific American*: "Mosses"; *Sierra* (US): "Aubade Now of Earth"; *Terrain.org*: "Solstice," "I asked to be lush, to be green.," "My Failure"; *The Threepenny Review*: "To Be a Person," "Two Versions"; *The Times Literary Supplement* (UK): "Aubade Now of Earth"; *VOX.com*: "Counting, New Year's Morning, What Powers Yet Remain to Me."

ANTHOLOGIES: *Alone Together: Love, Grief, and Comfort During the Time of Covid-19*: "Today, When I Could Do Nothing"; *And We Came Outside and Saw the Stars Again*: "Today, When I Could Do Nothing"; *Beat Not Beat*: "Counting, New Year's Morning, What Powers Yet Remain to Me"; *Earth Song*: "Today, When I Could Do Nothing"; *Pandemic Puzzle Poems*: "Today, When I Could Do Nothing"; *The Path to Kindness: Poems of Connection and Joy*: "I Would Like"; *The Wonder of Small Things: Poems of Peace & Renewal*: "Solstice"; *Together in a Sudden Strangeness: American Poets Respond to the Pandemic*: "Today, When I Could Do Nothing."

Index of titles

335

Jane Hirshfield, born in New York City and a longtime resident of northern California, is the author of ten collections of poetry, including *The Asking: New & Selected Poems* (US, Knopf, 2023; UK, Bloodaxe Books, 2024) and an earlier retrospective, *Each Happiness Ringed by Lions* (Bloodaxe Books, 2005). Her 2006 collection, *After*, was a Poetry Book Society Choice and shortlisted for the T.S. Eliot Prize. Called 'one of the most important writers in the world today' (*The New York Times Magazine*) and one of American poetry's central spokespersons for the biosphere, she is the founder of an online and travelling interactive exhibit exploring the alliance of poetry and science. Also the author of *Hiddenness, Surprise, Uncertainty: Three Generative Energies of Poetry* (Newcastle/Bloodaxe Poetry Lectures, 2008) and two now-classic US collections of essays, *Nine Gates: Entering the Mind of Poetry* (1997) and *Ten Windows: How Great Poems Transform the World* (2015), she has edited and co-translated four books presenting the work of world poets from the deep past: the anthology *Women in Praise of the Sacred: 43 Centuries of Spiritual Poetry by Women* (1994); *The Ink Dark Moon: Poems by Ono No Komachi and Izumi Shikibu* (US, 1988; UK 2023) and *The Heart of Haiku* (2011), both with Mariko Aratani; and *Mirabai: Ecstatic Poems* (2004), with Robert Bly. Her own poetry has been translated into seventeen languages, including by Czesław Miłosz, who wrote the introduction to her 2002 Polish Selected Poems. Recipient of numerous literary awards, an elected member of the American Academy of Arts & Sciences, and a former chancellor of the Academy of American Poets, she has taught at Stanford University, U.C. Berkeley, and elsewhere, and was the 2022 Seamus Heaney International Visiting Poetry Fellow at Queen's University, Belfast.

MIX
Paper | Supporting
responsible forestry
FSC® C007785
FSC
www.fsc.org